CAMBRIDGE LIBRARY COLLECTION

Books of enduring scholarly value

Travel and Exploration

The history of travel writing dates back to the Bible, Caesar, the Vikings and the Crusaders, and its many themes include war, trade, science and recreation. Explorers from Columbus to Cook charted lands not previously visited by Western travellers, and were followed by merchants, missionaries, and colonists, who wrote accounts of their experiences. The development of steam power in the nineteenth century provided opportunities for increasing numbers of 'ordinary' people to travel further, more economically, and more safely, and resulted in great enthusiasm for travel writing among the reading public. Works included in this series range from first-hand descriptions of previously unrecorded places, to literary accounts of the strange habits of foreigners, to examples of the burgeoning numbers of guidebooks produced to satisfy the needs of a new kind of traveller - the tourist.

The Discovery and Settlement of Port Mackay, Queensland

Port Mackay is a district of Queensland, Australia, best known for its production of cane sugar. It was first settled in the 1860s, when John Mackay (1839–1914) successfully completed a mission to claim farmland and introduce agriculture there. First published in 1908, this study by the businessman and keen amateur anthropologist Henry Ling Roth (1855–1925) explores the district's history, tracing its development from an uncharted territory barely noticed by early European explorers to a burgeoning community that profited from its ideal conditions for cultivation. Drawing on extensive notes from his visits to the region over thirty years, as well as some fascinating anecdotal accounts from settlers, Roth explores the achievements of Port Mackay's early colonists in agriculture, industry and sea trading. The book contains maps and photographs, and includes a short account of the local Aboriginal population, and substantial notes on natural history and sporting pursuits.

T0352389

Cambridge University Press has long been a pioneer in the reissuing of out-of-print titles from its own backlist, producing digital reprints of books that are still sought after by scholars and students but could not be reprinted economically using traditional technology. The Cambridge Library Collection extends this activity to a wider range of books which are still of importance to researchers and professionals, either for the source material they contain, or as landmarks in the history of their academic discipline.

Drawing from the world-renowned collections in the Cambridge University Library, and guided by the advice of experts in each subject area, Cambridge University Press is using state-of-the-art scanning machines in its own Printing House to capture the content of each book selected for inclusion. The files are processed to give a consistently clear, crisp image, and the books finished to the high quality standard for which the Press is recognised around the world. The latest print-on-demand technology ensures that the books will remain available indefinitely, and that orders for single or multiple copies can quickly be supplied.

The Cambridge Library Collection will bring back to life books of enduring scholarly value (including out-of-copyright works originally issued by other publishers) across a wide range of disciplines in the humanities and social sciences and in science and technology.

The Discovery
and Settlement
of Port Mackay,
Queensland

Henry Ling Roth

CAMBRIDGE
UNIVERSITY PRESS

CAMBRIDGE UNIVERSITY PRESS

Cambridge, New York, Melbourne, Madrid, Cape Town,
Singapore, São Paolo, Delhi, Tokyo, Mexico City

Published in the United States of America by Cambridge University Press, New York

www.cambridge.org
Information on this title: www.cambridge.org/9781108039338

© in this compilation Cambridge University Press 2011

This edition first published 1908
This digitally printed version 2011

ISBN 978-1-108-03933-8 Paperback

PORT MACKAY, QUEENSLAND.

FRONTISPIECE.—Habana Creek. E. M. Long in the foreground. From a photograph by G. H. M. King (Fryerne) taken in 1887.

THE

DISCOVERY AND SETTLEMENT

OF

Port Mackay, Queensland

WITH NUMEROUS ILLUSTRATIONS,
CHARTS AND MAPS,
AND SOME NOTES ON THE NATURAL HISTORY
OF THE DISTRICT

BY

H. LING ROTH

At one time Hon. Sec. of the Mackay Planters' and Farmers' Association.
Author of "A Guide to the Literature of Sugar;"
"The Aborigines of Tasmania;"
"The Natives of Sarawak and British North Borneo;"
"Great Benin: Its Customs, Art and Horrors;"
&c., &c.

1908.

HALIFAX, ENGLAND,

F. KING & SONS, Ltd.,

AND ALL BOOKSELLERS.

ERRATA.

PREFACE.

THE collection of notes for this little work was begun some thirty years ago, when I went out to Port Mackay, and originated in the fact that it was at all times difficult to get authentic information as to the discovery of the country, and as to the doings of the colonists who settled it. The first local newspaper, *The Mackay Mercury*, was started in 1866, but as the editor, when he afterwards left the district, carried away with him all copies of the paper up to the beginning of 1867, it may be said there are no printed records earlier than 1867. A year or two ago the proprietors of the *Mercury* published a *resumé* of events from the first of January, 1867 onwards. I have, therefore, only dealt with the district's history up to that year.

Besides my own notes, I am indebted to other colonists for information which is acknowledged in the text. Apart from these, a very thorough search has been made at the British Museum and the Record Office (Admiralty and Colonial Papers) for any particulars which might throw further light on the doings of the early explorers on the coast, or which might confirm what has been published elsewhere. Notes so obtained have been incorporated in the work.

The book being essentially prepared for Queensland readers, who in many cases have not easy access to books of travel, such as those of Cook, Flinders, King, etc., which deal with the coast of the Mackay District, and of others, which, like *Leichhardt's Journal*, are not often met with even in Second-hand Book Circulars (when I was in Mackay there was only one copy, and that was in the hands of M. Hume Black, M.L.A.), I have, where it seemed to me to be necessary, given fairly full extracts from these works, so that the local readers can have their information as much at first hand as is possible.

It may at first sight seem to be stretching a point a little by quoting travels so far in land as those of Leichhardt, but Leichhardt's journey led him within the watershed from which wool was sent down to Port Mackay for shipment, when the Pioneer River was discovered, which watershed still remains largely within the sphere of the Port's activities.

Some of the illustrations are from photographs, mostly made by Boag and Mills (afterwards Reckitt and Mills), which I brought home with me, others are from photographs taken by my friends C. C. Rawson, G. H. M. King and E. J. Welch, and others have been lent me by J. Ewen Davidson. Some of the older ones dating back to 1866 have not come out so clearly as they might have done, because a clayed surface paper has not been used—the work being mainly intended for use in the tropics and semi-tropics, where such paper quickly deteriorates. The illustrations from photographs are of the year 1866 and onwards.

For the guidance of Home readers, explanatory notes have been inserted where it seemed to me they are required.

H. LING ROTH.

ROYAL COLONIAL INSTITUTE,
LONDON, *25th February, 1908.*

CONTENTS.

LIST OF ILLUSTRATIONS.

FRONTISPIECE—HABANA CREEK.　From a photograph by G. H. M. KING.

MAPS AND CHARTS.

INTRODUCTION.

Port Mackay is situated in Lat. 21° 9′ S, Long. 149° 14′ E, and its site with the surrounding country was discovered by Captain John Mackay in 1860, the curious part about the discovery being the fact that the district had remained unknown until the country to the South, West and North had been discovered, and more or less settled. The link between Leichhardt's track, the only *early* land track approaching the district, and Captain Mackay's is as follows:—A. C. Gregory, coming from the Gulf Country in 1856, touched Leichhardt's line of exploration, and then continued his southern course until he arrived at Conner and Fitz's Station, on the Dawson River; Conner afterwards moving up north, to Princhester, where he was in 1859 overtaken by Captain Mackay.

The District of Port Mackay is the chief seat of the Sugar Industry in Queensland, and is inhabited by a class of people who are second to none in Australia for "go-aheadedness." On one occasion, when the Government declined to grant them certain reforms, they elected John Bright to represent them in the Legislative Assembly, an honour he naturally declined; but they have always returned men to Parliament who have left their mark on the legislation of the State. It was, on the carefully prepared representation of a Mackay Planter, G. H. M. King, that the late Sir Thomas McIlwraith hoisted the British Flag in New Guinea. The coast of this District was at one time noted for its Dugong Fishery, carried on by a Devonshire gentleman named Ching. Mackay was once the home of Madame Melba.

It enjoys a delightful semi-tropical climate, and is surrounded by a fairly high range of forest covered hills from which lovely views may be had, not only of the country itself, but also of the islands which dot the coast where Captain Cook pluckily steered his craft 139 years ago.

THE DISCOVERY AND SETTLEMENT OF PORT MACKAY, QUEENSLAND.

CHAPTER I.

THE EARLY DISCOVERIES ON THE EAST COAST OF AUSTRALIA, 1770—1844.

The discovery of the East Coast of Australia, where Port Mackay is situated, was the achievement of the great navigator, Captain James Cook, R.N., F.R.S. After completing his arduous duties on the coast of North America,* he was chosen as the Commander of the Expedition destined to observe the transit of Venus at Tahiti, one of the Society Islands. This Island, which is believed to have been discovered by Quiros, in 1606, had been discovered independently by Capt. Wallis in the "Dolphin," in 1767. Cook started from the River Thames on the 21st July, 1768, in H.M. barque the "Endeavour," going out via the Cape of Good Hope. On completing his work at the Society Islands, he circumnavigated New Zealand and arrived off the coast of Australia at a place he named Point Hicks, after his first lieutenant, who discovered it on the 19th April, 1770. Then he discovered Botany Bay, where he stayed several days, and on the 6th May he started on his ever memorable journey of discovery up the coast. On the 29th May he anchored in Thirsty Sound, which he so named on account of the crew's inability to find fresh water there, and on May 31st he anchored in Broadsound. He passed and named Cape Palmerston, after Henry, Viscount Palmerston, Lord of the Admiralty and on the 1st June was due east of Cape Hillsborough, which he so named after the Earl of Hillsborough, who was First Secretary of State for the Colonies, and President of the Board of Trade, when the "Endeavour" sailed.† Of the aspect of the country here he says: "The Main Land is here pretty much diversified with Mountains, Hills, plains and Vallies, and seem'd to be tollerably Cloathed with Wood and Verdure. These Islands [the Cumberland Islands] which lay Parrallel with the coast, and from 5 to 8 or 9 Leagues off, are of Various Extent, both for height and circuit; hardly any Exceeds 5 Leagues in Circuit are very small. Besides the chain of Islands, which lay at a distance from the coast, there are other Small Ones laying under the Land. Some few smokes were seen on the Main land." On the 3rd June he was obliged to anchor in a bay, which he named Repulse Bay, as he found by the tides there was no further passage there to the N.W.; he then rounded Cape Conway, so named after General H. S. Conway, who was Secretary of State

* See Arthur Kitson's *Capt. James Cook*, London, 1907.

† See Admiral Wharton's *Capt. Cook's Journal*, London, 1893.

1765-68, and on the 4th steered through Whitsunday Passage.* Of the Passage Cook writes: "Our Depth of water in running thro' was between 25 & 20 fathoms; everywhere good anchorage; indeed the whole passage is one Continued safe Harbour, besides a Number of small Bays and Coves on each side, where ships may lay as it were in a Bason: at least so it appear'd to me, for I did not wait to Examine it . . . . The land, both on the Main and Islands, especially the former, is Tolerably high, and distinguished by Hills and Vallies, which are diversified with Woods and Lawns that looked green and pleasant. On a Sandy Beach upon one of the Islands we saw 2 people and a Canoe, with an outrigger, which appeared to be both Larger and differently built to any we have seen upon the Coast. . . . This passage I have named Whitsunday's Passage, as it was discover'd on the day the Church commem-

Fig. 1.—Ll. Island Cumberland Group. From a Sketch taken by one of the artists on board the "Endeavour." In the British Museum this sketch is included in Buchan's collection; but Buchan died 17 April, 1769, at Tahiti, twelve months before Cook was off the East Coast of New Holland. The sketch is probably by John Reynolds.

orates that Festival, and the Isles which form it Cumberland Isles, in honour of H.R.H. the Duke of Cumberland after Hy. Fredk. Duke of Cumberland, a younger brother of George III." He also named Cape Gloucester after Wm. Hy. Duke Duke of Glo'ster & Edinburgh, another younger brother of the same King. Then he passed northward, away from what is now known as the Mackay district, and although he made two more voyages of discovery he did not revisit this coast.

Cook left many inlets and islands unsurveyed, but it must be remembered his survey was a first one, and the wonder is that considering the innumerable shoals, rocks, &c., he had to contend against, he managed so well as he did, both as regards the accuracy and general excellence of his surveys and his successful navigation of this and other seas.†

* This Passage is quite the equal in beauty of the Bocus so justly belauded by Chas. Kingsley in *Westward Ho!* I have passed through both Straits during daylight in fine weather.—H.L.R.

† Admiral Wharton, himself a distinguished hydrographer, eulogises Cook's work in the highest terms, and Prof. Dr. Carl E. Meinicke speaks of "the usual care and thoroughness" with which Cook did his surveys. (*Die Inseln des Stillen Oceans*, Leipzig, 2nd Ed., 1888.)

The discovery of Botany Bay by Capt. Cook led very quickly to the first European settlements in Australia (1788), and these in turn, together with the increasing desire to make further discoveries, was the cause of the continued navigation of these Seas.   But apart from adventurous sailors of whose doings there are no records, or of the surveyors specially employed, there were others who sailed up the coast and added a pathetic touch to the rough life of those times.   On or about May, 1791, the time expired convict, Wm. Bryant, and his wife Mary with their two children, one an infant at the breast, Jas. Cox, Wm. Allen, Nath. Lilly, Jas. Martin, Sam Bird, Sam Brown and Wm. Morton, all convicts, passed up the coast from Port Jackson, Sydney, to Timor in a boat 22ft. long.   At Timor some of them died; one was drowned at Sunda; the rest were handed over to the British authorities, carried to England, and sentenced at Newgate to complete their sentences.

In 1793 the "Hormazeer," Captain Wm. Brampton, bound from Norfolk Island to Bombay, passed up the coast, incidentally discovered the Brampton Shoals, and lost part of a boat's crew, killed by the natives on Darnley's Island.   She was accompanied by the "Chesterfield," Captain Mathew B. Alt.   In 1798 the ship "Eliza," Captain Swain, went up the coast, following somewhat the track of the brig "Deptford," Capt. Campbell, which in 1797 struck on a reef near long. 151° in almost the same latitude as that of Cape Palmerston.   According to the Log of the "Lady Nelson," 6th Oct., Campbell and Swain laid down this reef two degrees off the nearest land instead of twenty miles.   Naturally as this route to China and the East Indies became better known the sailings along the coast increased annually with the augmenting immigrant population, but the next voyage of historical importance was that of Capt. Matthew Flinders, R.N., a man of whom all Australians ought to be proud.   He was grandfather* of Prof. Flinders Petrie, F.R.S., the Egyptologist, and was born at Spalding, Lincolnshire, England, in 1774.   He had served under Captain Bligh in the "Providence" in 1791, and had come out to Australia the first time with Vice-Admiral Hunter, on his second voyage in 1795.

Capt. Flinders, who had already explored the East Coast of Australia as far north as Hervey's Bay, left Sydney on the 22nd July, 1802, on a voyage of discovery in H.M. Sloop "Investigator," accompanied by the "Lady Nelson."   In his quest was also included the finding of any clue which would lead to the discovery of the fate of the missing Expedition of La Perouse.   On the 4th August he discovered Port Curtis† which he so named after Sir Roger Curtis, the Commandant at the Cape of Good Hope, who had taken a lively interest in Flinders' work and had been of considerable assistance to him.   On the 9th September he located Mount Funnel and so named it "from its form."   On the 28th Sept. he writes "we steered for the north-easter-most of the Northumberland Islands, which I intended to visit in the way to Torres Straits. These are no otherwise marked by Capt. Cook, than as a single piece of land indistinctly seen, of three leagues in extent; but I had already described from Mount Westall and Pier Head a cluster of islands, forming a distinct portion of this archipelago; and in honour of the noble house to which Northumberland gives the

* Through his only child Anne.

† Mr. J. P. Hogan, M.P., in his *Gladstone* [*Port Curtis*] *Colony*, Lond., 1898, p. 3, quotes Cardinal Moran as identifying Port Curtis as the spot where Quiros landed in Australia in 1606! Needless to say Quiros never got nearer to this part of Australia than the New Hebrides.   The Island Espiritu Santo of this group is generally considered by geographers to have been discovered by that navigator.

title of Duke, I named them Percy Islands." Of No. 2 Percy Isle, the largest of them, being about thirteen miles in circumference with a greater elevation of perhaps a thousand feet, Flinders says : " The surface of the island is either sandy or stony, or both, with a small proportion of vegetable soil intermixed. It is generally

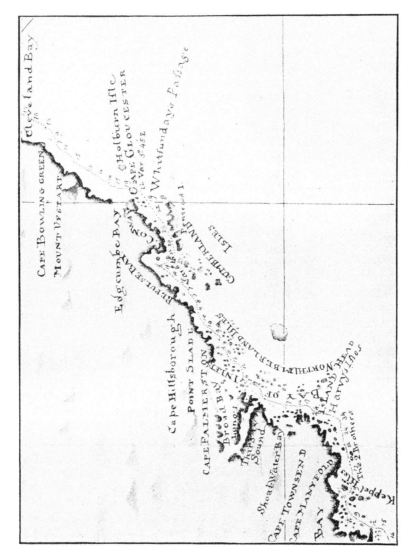

Fig. 2.—Facsimile of Captain Cook's Rough Chart of Part of the East Coast of New Holland. British Museum.

covered with grass and wood; and some of the valleys round the basin might be made to produce vegetables, especially one in which there was a small run, and several holes of fresh water. The principal wood is the *Eucalyptus*, or Gum tree, but it is not large ; small cabbage palms grow in the gullies, and also a species of

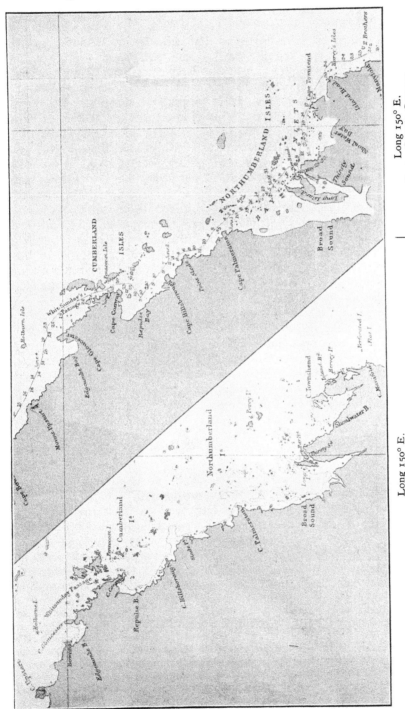

Fig. 3.—Two Charts of the Queensland Coast covering the Mackay District, to shew the general accuracy of Capt. Cook's Surveys. Reproduced, by permission of Elliott Stock, from Admiral Wharton's Edition of *Capt. Cook's Journal during his First Voyage round the World.* London (Elliott Stock) 1893.

Fig tree, which bears its fruit on the stem, instead of the ends of the branches; and Pines are scattered in the most rocky places." No inhabitants were seen upon any of the Percy Islands, but there were deserted fire places upon all. The Indians probably come over from the mainland at certain times to take turtle, in which they must be more dexterous than we were, for although many turtle were seen in the water, and we watched the beaches at night, not one was caught. There are no kanguroos upon the Percy Isles; nor did we see any useful birds. The large bats, or vampyres, common to this country, and called flying foxes at Port Jackson, were often found hanging by the claws, with their heads downward, under the shady tops of the palm trees; and one solitary eel of a good size was caught on clearing out the pool where our water casks had been first intended to fill. Pines, fresh water and fish will be some inducement to visit the Percy Isles; as perhaps may be the hump-backed whales, of which a considerable number was seen in the vicinity. . . . A wet dock might be made of the basin without other trouble or expense than a little deepening of the narrow entrance, and throwing a pair of gates across; and were the mud to be cleared out the basin would contain fifteen or twenty sail of merchant ships with great ease." The basin referred to is situated in the channel between No. 2 and the western pine islets. On the 16th October Flinders landed on the Cumberland Islands, and on the 18th of the same month the "Lady Nelson" returned to Port Jackson and Flinders continued his investigations northward. He then circumnavigated Australia and returned to Port Jackson on the 9th June, 1803.

With the "Lady Nelson" was sent back the naturalist, Robert Brown, much to his regret and our disappointment, for in so far as our present enquiry extends he had only landed at one each of the Northumberland and Cumberland Isles. When he was returned to Sydney he wrote to Sir Chas. Greville expressing his dissatisfaction as follows, 7 Aug., 1703: "Capt. Flinders who does not rate the importance of such collections [Flora, seeds, &c.] very high thought I suppose he did enough in affording me opportunities of landing at our different anchorages; the trouble of ordering boxes to be made [&c., &c., &c.] he does not seem to have reckoned on. I would rather attribute his conduct to his total inexperience in such matters than to any other cause." A search amongst the letters of Brown to Sir Jos. Banks, P.R.S., does not throw any further light on the matter.

On the 10th August Flinders started home as a passenger in the sloop "Porpoise," Lieut. Fowler of the "Investigator" in command. They were accompanied by the "Cato," Capt. John Park, and the East Indiaman "Bridgewater," Captain E. H. Palmer. On the 17th of August the "Porpoise" and "Cato" were wrecked—the "Bridgewater" sailing away without offering to help in any way. The wrecked crews got on to a sandbank, a cutter was manned and in it Flinders sailed south for succour. On the 7th October Flinders was back at Wreck Reef* and Cato Bank in the schooner "Cumberland," 29 tons, built at

---

* Wreck Reef Bank is thus described by Flinders:—" It is about twenty miles long, and from a quarter, to one mile and a half in breadth; and consists of many distinct patches of different magnitudes, the six principal of which are from four to eight or ten miles in circuit. They are separated by channels of one mile to near a league in width; and in the two eastmost I found from eight to ten fathoms, and nothing to prevent a ship passing through in a case of necessity. Four of the six larger patches have each a sandbank near the middle, which do not appear to have been lately covered by the tide; and they were now more or less frequented by sea birds, such as Noddies,

Port Jackson, accompanied by the ship "Rolla," Capt. Rob. Cumming, and the schooner "Francis," Capt. Jas. Aiken. The last named returned with some passengers and stores to Sydney, the "Rolla" went on to China, and the "Cumberland" proceeded home via Torres Straits, but, with her commander, passengers and crew, were made prisoners at the Mauritius. So ended Flinders' career as an explorer of the very highest ability. He was the first to suggest the name of "Australia," for the island continent which up to then had not been honoured with a collective title.

In 1812 Captain Cripps in the brig "Cyclops" passed up the coast from Port Jackson to Bengal. He took the inner route, *i.e.*, the route inside the Great Barrier Reef. He made the land at Buzzard's Bay and then followed Cook's tracks, and must therefore have sailed close along the Mackay Coast. In this year the Frederic Reef was discovered by a ship of that name; here the "Queen Charlotte" was wrecked in 1825 (?).

Three years later, on April 19th, 1815, Lieut. Jeffries in H.M. Brig "Kangaroo" sailed from Port Jackson, bound to Ceylon, with a detachment of troops. Having thick weather as Wreck Reef was approached, rendering it unpleasant to run for the narrow channels of the Barrier Reefs, the passage inside of the Great Barrier Reefs, was therefore pursued. On April 28th the brig rounded Break Sea-Spit, and filled up her water at Port Bowen,† where she was detained several days by a gale of wind. From here the track of Captain Cook was followed, as nearly as possible, inside of Northumberland and Cumberland Islands, through Whitsunday Passage. In July of this year the "Indefatigable" passed up, taking the outer route, being accompanied by the "Cochin," a small ship and a brig. In this year also the "Lady Elliott," a merchant ship, got into low water at Shoal Point.

In 1817, Captain Brodie, in the "Alert," passed up on his way from Port Jackson to Calcutta. Some twelve months later, in September, 1818, the ships "Claudine," Captain J. Welch, and "Mary," Captain Ormond, sailed past, bound from Port Jackson to Batavia, and discovered what has since been known as the Claudine Entrance in the Great Barrier Reef. About three months previous to this, on the 21st June, 1818, Captain R. Carns discovered Carns or Mid-day Reef, in the ship "Neptune," from Port Jackson, bound to Calcutta. In July of this year, Captain Bell, of the "Minerva," passed up on the way to India.

In 1819 a Capt. Howard, from Tasmania, had freighted the "Frederick"‡ and the "Wellington" with sheep and cattle for the Isle of France (Mauritius), a market

---

Boobies, Tropic, and Man-of-War birds, Gamuts, and perhaps some others. Of these four banks, two lie to the west and one to the east of that near which our ship struck; but the eastern bank is the most considerable, and most frequented by birds. Turtle also land there occasionally, and this bank was not improperly called Bird Islet, being now covered with coarse grass, some shrubs, and a soil to which the birds are every day making an increase . . . . Besides sea birds of the species already mentioned they procured many thousand eggs; and also four turtle, of which one weighed 459 pounds, and contained so many eggs, that Lieutenant Fowler's journal says: ' no less than 1940, large and small, were counted.' " The position of Wreck Reef Bank is Latitude 22° 11′ 23″ S. Longitude 155° 18′ 50,″5 E.

† Discovered by Flinders in August, 1802, and so named by him in compliment to Capt. Jas. Bowen, of the Navy, and not to be confounded with Bowen, Port Denison, discovered by Sinclair and Gordon in 1859.

‡ One is inclined to ask whether this was the vessel that discovered the Frederick Reef, in 1812. There was another "Frederic," of this convicts got possession in 1834 and sailed in her to South America.

which then offered large profits. After some delay they reached the Northumberland Islands off which the stock all died from want of room and influence of climate. Unwilling to proceed without cargo, the Captain* detained the vessels for spars. On proceeding she was wrecked off Clack Island, Cape Melville, and twenty-two of the crew were drowned; but the chief officer, one woman and a boy reached the "Wellington." Going on to Timor and thence to Batavia the Captain died, the crew dispersed, "the vessel was taken under charge by the Orphan Chamber, her register being lost and her owners unknown." In August of this year (1819) the "Baring," Captain Lamb, from Port Jackson to India, sailed up the coast.

On the 3rd June of the same year, Lieut. Phillip Parker King, son of Governor King, watered on No. 1 Percy Islands. He began his Survey where Flinders left off (*Colonial Corr. N. S. Wales, Vol. 95*). On the 5th of the month he and his crew kept the King of England's (William IV.) birthday there. "Tracks of natives, but not of recent date, were noticed. In our walks over the hills we saw abundance of quails, but no animals were observed; very few sea birds frequented the beaches, perhaps on account of the contiguity of the barrier reefs, upon which they can much more plentifully procure their food. On the hills, which are very rocky, the grass grew luxuriantly, although the soil is shallow and poor; but in the gullies Mr. Cunningham found some good loamy ground, in which he sowed a few peach stones, which would doubtless thrive were it not for the fires of the natives. We saw very few pine trees that exceeded forty feet in height, and the cones were not yet formed. Mr. Cunningham remarked a great similarity between the botanical productions of this part and of the north coast, although there is a difference in latitude of 10°." They passed the Beverley group the same night, and after being becalmed were at Point Slade on the 7th June, rounded Cape Hillsborough, and anchored in Repulse Bay. Of Cape Hillsborough, King remarks:—"The country in the vicinity, and particularly to the southward of the Cape, is rocky and mountainous; but the lower grounds are verdant, well clothed with timber; and, judging from the numerous fires along the coast, it must be very populous; the islands near it are rocky and very barren, but many of them being wooded with pine have a picturesque appearance." On the 8th June, 1819, he named the Repulse Isles, describing them as follows:— "These islets are furnished with a very poor and shallow soil. On the sides of the hills we noticed a species of *Xanthorhœa*, remarkable for its stunted growth and for the curly habit of its leaves. Pumice stone was found at the foot of the hills, washed up, perhaps, by the tide; and on the beach was an European ashen oar. Under the projecting rocks several firing and sleeping places were observed, which had been recently occupied by natives." On the 9th June he rounded Cape Conway and tells us this Cape "is formed by steep rocky hills, rising to the height of nearly 800 feet above the sea; the sides of which were so steep, and so impenetrably covered by a thick underwood, that we could not accomplish its ascent; we were therefore obliged to confine our observations to the beach. Tracks of natives were observed, and either a wrecked or worn out canoe, made of bark, was lying near the ruins of two or three bark huts." In writing to Governor Goulbourn, King mentions with some pride "At Endeavour river I remained a fortnight occupying the very place that Capt. Cook used when he was there in 1770." Continuing his circumnavigation of Australia, King got back to Port Jackson on 12th January, 1820. His vessel was the

* This was not Captain Howard, who had already been wrecked on Cape Barren. West's *History of Tasmania*, I. p. 75.

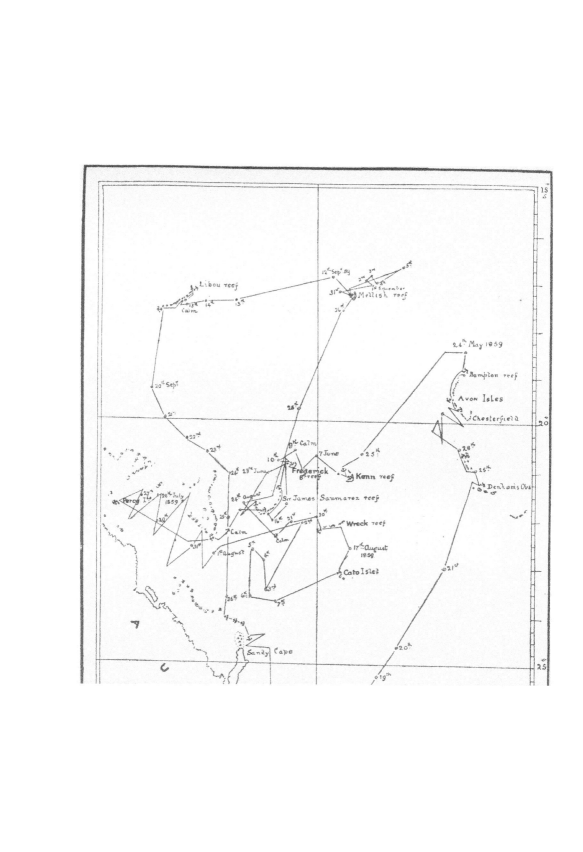

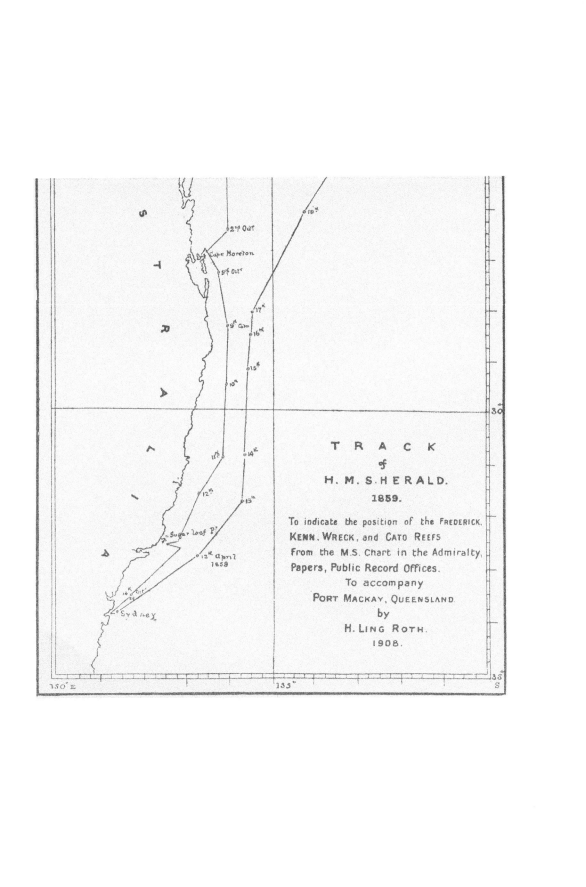

T R A C K
of
H. M. S. HERALD.
1859.

To indicate the position of the FREDERICK.
KENN. WRECK, and CATO REEFS
From the M.S. Chart in the Admiralty.
Papers, Public Record Offices.
To accompany
PORT MACKAY, QUEENSLAND
by
H. LING ROTH.
1908.

teak cutter, the "Mermaid," of 84 tons burthen. This voyage was his second one of importance.

King then made a third voyage, this time passing the Percy Isles on the 23—24 July, 1820, naming Mount Dryander, after Jonas Dryander, a celebrated Swedish naturalist, lately deceased, the height of which he placed at 4566 feet.* In his Sailing Directions King remarks as follows on Mount Dryander. "At the back of Point Slade there is a high mountainous range extending without interruption to the westward of Mount Upstart. In latitude 21°1½ and longitude 148°36¾ is a high rounded summit, which is visible at a distance of twenty leagues; between this range, which is at a distance of from five to seven leagues from the sea, and the coast, are several ridges gradually lowering in altitude as they approach the shore. In the neighbourhood of Repulse Bay, this mountainous range recedes, and has a considerable track of low land at its base, which is possibly a rich country; from the height of the hills it must be well watered." The Cumberland Islands King describes as all high and rocky, "they are covered on their windward or south-east sides with stunted timber and pine trees; but the leeward sides, being sheltered from the wind, are generally well clothed with grass and timber." He does not speak well of the timber on this occasion, as being too knotty, but as we shall see directly, he changed his opinion of it later on. King then circumnavigated Australia once more, arriving at Port Jackson on the 9th December, 1820. However by the beginning of June, 1821, he was again off this coast. This fourth voyage was made in the 170 ton teak brig, the "Bathurst," so re-named by Governor Macquarie, and on this occasion he was accompanied part of the way by the "Dick" and "San Antonio" merchantmen on their way to Batavia.

Of Percy Island No. 2, where he anchored on the 10th June, he says:—"This Island, like No. 1, which we visited in 1819, appears to be principally of quartzose formation. The soil is sandy, and affords but little nourishment to the stunted trees with which it is furnished. In the more barren and rocky parts the pine was abundant, but not growing to any great size. The 'Dick's' people cut down and embarked several logs; on examination they were thought to be useless; but from subsequent experience, they proved to be far from deserving such contempt, for during the voyage we made two pole-top gallant masts of it; which, although very full of knots, were as tough as any spar I ever saw; and carried a press of sail longer than would be trusted on many masts. These trees are very abundant on the Cumberland and Northumberland Islands, but do not attain any large size; being seldom higher than 50 or 60 feet, or of a greater diameter than from 12 to 18 inches. Among a variety of birds, several black cockatoos and a pheasant cuckoo were seen. The beaches were frequented by gulls, terns, and oyster catchers; and an egret was noticed of a slate coloured plumage, with a small ruff upon its head. The seine was hauled upon the beach; but the only fish caught were two very large sting-rays; one of which measured 12 feet across; as it was too unwieldy to take on board, we had no means of weighing it; but the liver nearly filled a small pork barrel. It is very probable that our bad success may be attributed to the presence of these fish, for on board the 'Dick' several snappers were caught with the hook and line."

In these voyages King discovered rocks on the route at Northumberland and Percy Groups which had not been marked by Cook. At Shoal Point, where Cook

* On the Queensland maps of to-day the height is given as 2690 feet.

2

had touched on a sandbank and the "Lady Elliott" in 1815 had got into very shoal water, King made special investigations; but as the "Mermaid" passed within three miles of the Point and could not discover any signs of shoaler water, King thought their sandbank must be farther out. King was also of opinion that there might be communication by water between Edgecumbe Bay and Repulse Bay, but in this matter later investigations proved that Cook was correct and King was wrong.

In May, 1820, the ships "Claudine," Captain Welch, above referred to, and the "Marquis of Hastings" passed up, and in July, 1822, the "Mary Ann," Captain Warrington, accompanied by the "Almoreh" and "Richmond," are also recorded as having passed the Mackay Coast. Kenn's Reef, which appears to belong to the group of the Cato, Wreck, Carn, etc., was discovered by Capt. Alex. Shand on his passage from Port Jackson to Torres Strait on April 3rd, 1824. In 1825, the "Lalla Rookh," Capt. Hugh Steward, from Port Macquarie with convicts, made her appearance in these waters. It must not be supposed that the vessels chosen for mention were the only ones which went up the coast during the period under review. The vessels named are mostly those which have either discovered some new shoal, reef or island,* or which have some historical interest attached to their doings. Others no doubt followed earlier more or less in Cook's track, but the records have yet to be found.

The next survey of importance in these waters was that of Capt. J. Lort Stokes, R.N., in command of H.M.S. Beagle. The Beagle was a 10 gun brig of the old type of boats for those days, commonly known as "coffins," but she proved an excellent ship and had already been used for exploring and surveying purposes under Capt. R. Fitzroy on two voyages, in the former of which she had carried Chas. Darwin round the world. She had also been commanded by Capt. P. P. King, above referred to. On 22nd June, 1839, Capt. Stokes reports that "from Port Bowen we steered to pass between No. 1 and No. 2 of the Northumberland Isles, in order that we might lay down their outlines correctly, and also determine the positions of some small islets lying on the S.W. side of No. 1. The most remarkable land in sight in the morning was Mount Westall, named by Flinders after the talented artist who accompanied him, and which forms the highest part of the eastern shore of Shoal Water Bay. The soundings during the night were very regular, only varying from 30 to 33 fathoms with a soft, muddy bottom, mixed occasionally with which the lead brought up small stones. The summit of No. 1 of the Northumberland Isles forms a remarkable peak 720 feet high; a sandy bay on the west side promised good anchorage, and on its south-east and northern sides were some high detached rocks. The heights of the other parts of the group vary from two to six hundred feet. The crests of the western isles are covered with pine trees, which give them a curious jagged appearance. In the afternoon we passed in 34 fathoms, four miles from the eastern side of the Percy Isles, which enabled us to add their eastern extremity in the chart. The main land falling so much back soon after passing Port Bowen, we could form no idea of its character, but certainly what we had seen did not leave a favourable impression of its apparent fertility. Captains Flinders and King, having given a description of the Percy Isles, it will not be necessary for me to say anything about them, further than they are composed of a trap-like compound with an aspect of serpentine, and that either on them or the Northumberland Isles

---

* See Horsburgh's India Directory, 2 vols., London, 1827, for a detailed account of their voyages and discoveries, etc.

sandalwood has been found of late, and taken by a Tasmanian vessel to the China market.   Just before dark, the soundings decreased to 29 fathoms, Pine Peak of Percy Group, bearing S.W. 10 miles.   Our course was now shaped for Cape Gloucester, the extreme of the Cumberland Isles.   At midnight we passed nearly two miles from the N.E. side of K. of the Cumberland Group, in 27 fathoms, in which depth we continued till getting abreast of Pentecost Island, the next evening, the 24th, when it increased to 35 fathoms, but still on the same kind of green, sandy mud bottom. At 10 p.m. we passed about seven miles from Cape Gloucester, which at that part was nearly 1600 feet high.   I may here observe that the barometer was very high with these fresh S.E. winds and hazy weather, and rather low during the light N.W. winds, we experienced in the neighbourhood of Cape Capricorn."

After circumnavigating the Continent the " Beagle " was again off the coast, in 1841.   This time the grand old ship had on board Lieut. Graham Gore, R.N., a grandson of the Lieut. John Gore who was on board the " Endeavour " when Cook discovered this coast and who, on Cook's third voyage, took command of the expedition after Cook had been killed and his successor, Capt. Clarke, had died of consumption.

This last visit of the " Beagle " was quickly followed by H.M.S. "Fly," Capt. Blackwood, R.N. in command.   He had commenced the survey of the coast at Sandy Cape on 21st December, 1842, and had reached Latitude 21°, or just a little north of Cape Hillsborough, early in February, 1843.   He was then obliged to return to Port Bowen for repairs, but he was off West Hill on the 14th February, and stayed in the neighbourhood until the 13th March.   The ship wanted water and was unable to find it ; but Lieut. Yule, in the " Bramble " tender, found it in abundance a little to the north of Cape Hillsborough.   Jukes, who afterwards became celebrated as a geologist, was naturalist to this expedition, and writes as follows of their doings and of the country :—" March 13th.—Weighed and ran to the northward, anchoring in shoal water a little north of Cape Palmerston ; the surveying officers employed in laying down the coast] and the neighbouring islands.

" March 14th.—At daylight, Captain Blackwood, with Mr. Melville and myself, left the ship in the first gig to examine an opening in the shore like a harbour.   We passed a small headland of red quartzose rock, on which we landed for a short time, and then steered for an opening in the mangroves ahead, which, however, we soon found to be a mere shallow creek.   We then rounded another rocky headland, and landing on the inside of it, proceeded to the summit.   From this we looked over what appeared a very fine port, five or six miles deep and three miles wide, but surrounded by a thick belt of mangroves round its upper portion.   It was now high water, and we proceeded in good spirits to examine it, crossing in a N.W. direction.   To our great regret, however, we got nowhere more than five fathoms in sailing across, and this only in a few places, the usual depth being only three or four.   We steered for two grassy hills near the N.W. corner of the bay, and went first to examine an opening at the back of them, which we soon found, however, to be a mere shoal, muddy channel, winding among a great expanse of mangroves.   Returning, we rowed nearly round the hills into a sandy cove, in approaching which the boat got aground, and as the tide was rapidly falling, she was shortly high and dry.

" Meanwhile, we waded ashore, and got our things out of her on to the beach, where we camped for the night.   We shot a few small plovers on the beach to add to our dinner, and while it was being cooked, walked up the hills near us. These were grassy slopes, the open woodland having very fine long grass everywhere about it; but much of the lower and flatter spaces, and some of the hills, were occupied by dense jungle. In this jungle were tall trees, with dark, umbrageous foliage, very different from the light, thinly-leaved gum-trees, and having immense creepers and climbers, like great ropes, stretching from tree to tree, and hanging down and matting the underwood into an impenetrable thicket. When we reached the top of the hill, it was low water, and we saw our fine looking port had now hardly a drop of water over half its space, the tide having receded to its entrance, and left mere detached pools among the mud flats and sand banks of the inner portion. The belt of mangroves appeared to stretch a mile or two into the interior of the country, but there seemed to be a considerable space of fine grass land between them and the hills, which were here more broken and detached than they were to the south of West Hill. Having returned to our camp, and dined about sunset, we made preparations for sleeping quite securely on the beach, as a fine sea breeze was blowing on it, but before ten o'clock this unfortunately died away, and for the remainder of the night we lay sleepless and helpless, but not unrepining, victims to a numerous host of sand-flies and musquitoes. Compared to these pests, savage men or ferocious beasts are really slight evils, since they may be guarded against or overcome, while these plagues render life miserable, and paralyze all one's energies by continual irritation and long want of sleep, without either the dignity or excitement of danger.

"March 15th.—We found on the beach this morning the remains of a large dugong, which had been feasted on by the natives, consisting of the skull and part of the vertebræ and flippers; it was too much burnt, however, and broken to make it worth bringing away, although the flesh still adhered to it in some places. About six o'clock we continued our route along the north shore of the bay, shooting fifteen or sixteen plover out of a large flock as we proceeded. At the mouth of the bay we landed to ascend a green hill, forming its northern point, and saw thence another considerable indentation of the coast about two miles to the northward; and it being determined we should go and examine it, Melville and I decided to walk across while Captain Blackwood went round in the boat. We found the intermediate country a rich grassy woodland, the trees large and wide apart, and the grass so long and thick as considerably to impede our progress. In a hollow, just at the back of a mass of jungle, lying at the head of a small sandy cove, with a reef of rocks at each point of it, we found several deep holes and small pools of excellent fresh water; and immediately after, came on a round, bare, grassy hill, just over the south point of the little bay. From this hill the bay appeared about two miles wide, stretching four or five miles into the country, with several coves and rocky headlands on each side, but large beds of mangroves round its upper portion. The country around, with the exception of the mangrove swamps, was very beautiful; low green hills, rising in every direction, with grassy slopes and fine timber. At the back of this fresh and fertile looking country, and distant about ten miles, continued the bold ridge of hills running parallel with the coast, and probably 2 or 3000 feet in height. While we were looking at the view, the gig came round, and landed in a cove below us, and we hastened down to it. At the foot of the hill we crossed a small marsh, now dry, in which grew a very tall reed-like grass, large pieces of which had recently been pulled up by the roots, bare clods and the loose grass lying about in heaps. The root of this grass is probably eaten by the natives, and it was the only sign we saw of their presence, except some large smokes rising a few miles farther to the northward. We saw no animals, except a reddish-coloured rat among some stones on the beach, of which, however, I only succeeded in catching the young ones. We now crossed to the north shore of the bay, but though it was high water, we nowhere succeeded in finding a greater depth than four fathoms. We established ourselves for the night on a little sandy beach at the foot of a green hill, where was a small deep hollow that the boat would probably float in at low water, and enable us to ascertain the rise and fall of tide. This was found during the night to be 25 feet six inches, the moon not yet at the full. The spring tide rise and fall, therefore, is probably little less than 30 feet. Just before sunset, in a gap in the nearest range of hills, we could count three other ranges immediately behind it, the last very distant. Still I could not be sure that they were distinct ridges, as they might be only the projecting points of an indented table land; I am, however, inclined rather to look upon the hills as composed of parallel ranges than as a level table land.

" March 16th.—Though at breakfast this morning we consumed all our remaining stock of provisions, Captain Blackwood decided on running up the bay with the flood tide, to examine one or two considerable openings in the mangroves. We first tried one going in at the N.W. corner, but as it did not look promising, returned and went up one running due west. A very strong flood tide swept us rapidly up the inlet, which gradually narrowed and wound about for the first three or four miles, when we found ourselves near some rocky, woody hills, with steep banks, and the inlet having all the aspect of a river. We landed at one or two points, but could get no view for the trees; and proceeding, came on more mangrove flats, till at length our winding channel ended when about five yards wide and five feet deep, having a mangrove swamp on the right, a thick jungle ahead, and a steep bank of gravel, about twenty feet high, on our left hand. Climbing up this, we found a level grassy woodland, stretching away to S. and W. as far as we could see for the trees, and walking about half a mile, found one large and deep water-course and several smaller, leading towards the inlet. They were now all dry, but a little drain of fresh water came out of the jungle ahead of the boat. The small cliffs were composed of gravel; the lower part a confused heap of quartz pebbles the size of the fist, but the upper part of much finer materials, with layers of sand pretty well sorted and stratified, and of course horizontal. As we were under the necessity of going back immediately, in order to save the tide, as we had not much time for examination, and at half-past ten set out on our return. The ebb tide took us as rapidly down as the flood brought us up; and after passing a heavy sea on a shoal bar at the mouth of the bay, we made sail for the ship, which had now run down a few miles to the northward. The rocks about these two shoal bays were all rough slate, or greywacke, or quartz rock, with a dip to the west in the only spot where the stratification was discernible.

" March 17th, 18th.—Running slowly on along shore to Cape Hillsborough, visiting Li Cumberland Island on our way. This island exhibited a singular mass of rocks, looking as if made up of angular fragments of compact feldspar cemented together. Cape Hillsborough is a bold headland, 900 feet high, very steep nearly all round. Its base was composed of a singular assemblage of quartzose rocks, unstratified, and containing several imbedded minerals. The upper part is composed of stratified materials, in thick, well marked beds, dipping S.W. at an angle of 15°. On the inner side of the headland, accordingly, these rocks are found at the sea level.

In the cliff on the north side of the hill, about 300 feet from the summit, the stratified rock is white, earthy, pulverulent, easily decomposing, but pretty tough when in mass; much worn into hollows with overhanging blocks and ledges. It contains either angular fragments or worn crystals, of a green translucent mineral, like a dull variety of feldspar, but which may be olivine. Large round blocks of a black rock were also seen embedded in it, but in an inaccessible position. The materials, notwithstanding their regular stratification and dip, look very much as if of volcanic origin. In the country at the back were some singular small conical hills, capped by clusters of small basaltic columns." On the 25th March they anchored in Port Molle, at the N.W. end of Whitsunday Passage. The voyage was then continued northwards, but in the beginning of April, 1844, the Fly was again passing up the coast on her way to Java, etc.

Summing up his observations on this part of Australia, Jukes says:—"The tract of the coast between Broad Sound and Whitsunday Passage, or the parallels of 22°15 and 20°20, differs in some respects from any other part of the coast of Australia we visited. Its apparent fertility is greater; it is better supplied with fresh water, and the rise and fall of tide is much greater. A solid range of hills, of a pretty uniform height, cuts off from the interior a lower undulating strip of land 5 to 10 miles broad, the whole of which seems to be of a high average fertility for Australia; the grass was fine, close and abundant; the timber large sized and various in kind." He speaks of "excellent anchorage," and continues:—"As far as climate is concerned, almost any tropical production might be cultivated, but I have too little confidence in the nature of the soil of any part of Australia to recommend *that* as a source of profit." However he dilates on the great natural advantages of the district; and later on, while mentioning the high tides as being favourable to shipbuilding, he adds in a footnote:—"After twice circumnavigating Australia, and visiting all its Colonies, especially those of the southern coast, I look back upon this tract between 22° and 20° with still higher expectations than before, and certainly have never seen any part of Australia *near the sea* of equal fertility, or of nearly equally pleasant and agreeable aspect, or combining so many natural advantages."

Fig. 4.—The S.S. "Bronzewing" the tender which carried passengers to and from the mail steamers off Flat Top Island, Port Mackay, in the seventies and eighties.

CHAPTER II.

EAST COAST LAND EXPLORATION, 1813—1846.

It must not be thought that a survey of the coast was all the investigation that satisfied the local Government of the day or the rapidly rising public opinion of this Continent. Inland surveys were being carried on but under much greater difficulties than the nautical ones. On the coast a tempestuous and a calm season could be relied upon, but the irregular rainfall of the interior was a great drawback to successful exploration. Added to this was the opposition offered by the Blue Mountains which, for twenty-five years, until 1813, baffled all attempts to cross them. Allen Cunningham had discovered the Darling Downs in 1827, but not until 1840 did Patrick Leslie, of Collaroi, in the district of Cassalis, N. S. Wales, and his party become the first squatters to settle on the Downs. The Downs once reached, exploration went on by leaps and bounds. In 1842, Russell, Petrie* and others made their celebrated boat voyage from Brisbane, resulting in the discovery of Wide Bay and the Mary River. But with the expansion of squatting the ever present scarcity of labour made itself more severely felt, and the idea grew up that by means of overland communication with Port Essington Asiatic labour could be introduced. Not one of the settlers of whatever class had any notion of the enormous distance which separated them from this northernmost port, and in all probability the scheme would never have got beyond the initial stages of discussion had it not been for the enthusiasm of a young scientific Prussian who had been sojourning amongst the aborigines† in the southern districts, and who had found his way to the Darling Downs in 1843. This young man was Dr. Ludwig Leichhardt.

Leichhardt started on his memorable journey at the end of September, 1844, and found himself early in February of the following year at the back of the country which we now know as the Port Mackay district. From the 11th to the 14th February, he was on a creek which he named "Hugh's Creek after Hughs,‡ Esq., of Darling Downs." A creek which joins the Hughs he named Tombstone Creek on account of the fissures in the sandstone which had been cut out by the action of water into figures resembling tombstones. On returning to their encampment of the 12th some "Blackfellows were found bathing in the water-hole, but fled as soon as we made our appearance. The wood-duck (*Bernicla jubata*) abounded in

---

* *The Genesis of Queensland*, by Henry Stuart Russell, Sydney, 1888. Tom Petrie's *Reminiscences of Early Queensland*, Brisbane, 1904.

† The natives met with by Cook and by those who have since followed him, are commonly spoken of as the Aborigines of Australia, but it is most probable that the ancestors of these natives drove out the real Aborigines, a negroid race, the remnant of which we found and promptly exterminated in Tasmania. See *Aborigines of Tasmania* by H. Ling Roth, 2nd Ed., 1899.

‡ This name should have been written Hugh*es*—Henry Hughes, of Westbrook, Darling Downs, the life-long friend of Henry Stuart Russell.

the water-holes, and the swamp pheasant (*Centropus Phasianas*, Gould) was heard several times." The party were much troubled by a small black ant which bit severely. "A large yellow hornet with two black bands over the abdomen, was seen humming about the water-holes."* A crow was shot and roasted and found to be exceedingly tender, which we considered to be a great discovery. . . . . . . We again enjoyed some fine messes of *Portulaca*. On the 12th February, in the scrub, *Fusanus* was observed in fruit, and the *Stenochilus* and the White *Vilex* in blossom; from the latter the native bee extracts a most delicious honey." He also noticed a small tree with fruit like an acorn, with a sweet pericarp but bitter seeds on which, pigeons, cockatoos and crows fed. On the 13th February he came on to a watercourse which led to the deep, broad channel of a river, but now entirely dry. Thinking this river promised to be of importance, Leichhardt named it the "Isaacs" in acknowledgement of the kind support we received from F. Isaacs, Esq., of Darling Downs.† Leichhardt continues:—"When we were approaching the river the sound of a tomahawk was heard, and guided by the noise, we soon came in sight of three black women: two of whom were busily occupied in digging for roots, whilst the other, perched on the top of a high flooded gum tree, was chopping out either an opposum or a bee's nest. They no sooner perceived us than they began to scream most dreadfully, swinging their sticks, and beating the trees, as if we were wild beasts which they wished to frighten away. We made every possible sign of peace, but in vain; the two root diggers immediately ran off, and the lady in the tree refused to descend. When I asked for water, in the language of the natives of the country we had left—'Yarrai, yarrai,' she pointed down the river and answered 'Yarrai ya'; and we found afterwards that her information was correct. Upon reaching the tree we found an infant, swaddled in layers of tea tree bark, lying on the ground; and three or four large yams. A great number of men, boys and children, who had been attracted by the screams of their companions, now came running towards us; but on putting our horses into a sharp canter, and riding towards them, they retired into the scrub. The yams proved to be the tubers of a vine, with blue berries; both tubers and berries had the same pungent taste, but the former contained a watery juice, which was most welcome to our parched mouths." On the 15th February Leichhardt examined the range which he had "observed some days before and named Coxen's Peak and Range, in honour of Mr. Coxen,‡ of Darling Downs." Of his view from this peak, Leichhardt writes:—"To the northward ranges rose beyond ranges, and to the eastward the country seemed to be flat to a great extent, and bounded by distant mountains. To the southward the eye wandered over an unbroken line of horizon, with the exception of one blue distant elevation: this immense flat was one uninterrupted mass of forest without the slightest break. Narrow bands of scrub approached the river from the westward, and separated tracts of fine open forest country, amongst which patches of the Poplar-gum forest were readily distinguished by the brightness of their verdure. A river seemed to come from the south-west;

* See Appendix: Notes on some Australian *Hymenoptera Aculeata*.

† This name should be Isaac (without a final 's').—Fred Isaac was brother of Henry Isaac, at one time in squatting partnership with Henry Hughes, near West Maitland. Fred Isaac with his partner, Arthur Hodgson, followed Patrick Leslie to the Darling Downs in Sept., 1840. Leichhardt did not see the proof sheets of his book, hence these errors.

‡ This Mr. Coxen was no doubt Mr. Charles Coxen, of Jondaryan, for whom Henry Denis had taken up this station on the Darling Downs in 1840.

Mrs. G. H. M. King.   W. Napier and P. B. Brooke
                        E. M. Long.

Fig. 5.—Wiston Hill, Habana, Mackay.   From a photograph by G. H. M. King, taken in 1887.

the Isaacs came from the north-west, and was joined by a large creek from the northward. There was no smoke, no sign of water, no sign of the neighbourhood of the sea coast; but all was one immense sea of forest and scrub.*

"The great outlines of the geology of this interesting country were seen at one glance. Along the eastern edge of a basaltic tableland rose a series of domitic cones, stretching from south-east to north-west parallel to the coast. The whole extent of country between the range and the coast, seemed to be of sandstone, either horizontally stratified, or dipping off the range; with the exception of some local disturbances, where basalt had broken through it. Those isolated ranges, such as Coxen's Range—the abruptness of which seemed to indicate igneous origin—were entirely of sandstone. The various Porphyries, and Diorites, and Granitic, and Sienitic rocks, which characterize large districts along the eastern coast of Australia, were missing; not a pebble, except of sandstone, was found in the numerous creeks and watercourses. Pieces of silicified wood† were frequent in the bed of the Isaacs. The nature of the soil was easily distinguished by its vegetation: the Bastard Box and Poplar Gum grew on a stiff clay; the narrow-leaved Ironbark, the Bloodwood, and the Moreton Bay Ash on a lighter sandy soil, which was frequently rotten and undermined with numerous holes of the funnel ant. Noble trees of the Flooded-gum grew along the banks of the creeks and around the hollows, depending rather upon moisture than upon the nature of the soil. Fine Casuarinas were occasionally met with along the creeks; and the Forest Oak *(Casuarina torulosa),* together with Rusty-gum, were frequent on the sandy ridges.

"One should have expected that the prevailing winds during the day, would have been from the south-east, corresponding to the south-east trade winds; but, through-out the whole journey from Moreton Bay to the Isaacs I experienced, with but few exceptions, during the day, a cooling breeze from the north and north-east. The thunder-storms came principally from the south-west, west and north-west; but generally shewed an inclination to veer round to the northward.

"From Coxen's Range I returned to the river. Later in the day loud cries of Cockatoos attracted our notice, and, on going in their direction, we came to a water-hole in the bed of the river, at its junction with a large oak tree creek coming from the northward. This water-hole is in latitude 22° 11'; the natives had fenced it round with branches to prevent the sand from filling it up, and had dug small wells near it, evidently to obtain a purer and cooler water, by filtration through the sand. Pigeons *(Geophaps scripta, Gould.)* had formed a beaten track to its edge; and, the next morning, whilst enjoying our breakfast under the shade of a gigantic Flooded-gum tree, we were highly amused to see a flight of fifty or more Partridge, Pigeons, tripping along the sandy bed of the river, and descending to the water's edge, and returning after quenching their thirst, quite unconscious of the dangerous proximity of hungry ornithophagi. The cockatoos, however, observed us, and seemed to dispute our occupation of their waters, by hovering above the tops of the highest trees, and making the air resound with their screams; whilst numerous crows, attracted by a neighbouring bush fire, watched us more familiarly, and the dollar bird passed with its arrow-like flight from shade to shade." Still travelling up the

---

* Compare this description with the illustration prepared from G. H. M. King's photograph of Wiston Hill, at Port Mackay.

† Largly found in the neighbourhood and on the shores of Lake Elphinstone.—H.L.R.

river " we observed a great number of very large dead shells of *Limnæa* and *Paludina*, in the dry water-holes and melon-holes along the scrub; some of them not even bleached; but everything seemed to indicate this to be a more than usually dry season. In the morning we returned to the camp . . . . . . and we had to remain four days [to the 21st Feb.] before the provision [dried meat and fat] was fit for packing.

"February 22nd.—On a ride with Mr. Gilbert up the river we observed several large reedy holes in its bed, in which the Blackfellows had dug wells; they were still moist, and swarms of hornets were buzzing about them. About eight miles north-west from the junction of North Creek with the river, a large flight of cockatoos again invited us to some good water-holes extending along a scrubby rise. Large Bastard-box flats lie between North Creek and the river. About four miles from the camp, the country rises to the left of the river, and ranges and isolated hills are visible, which are probably surrounded by plains. Wherever I had an opportunity of examining the rocks I found sandstone; flint pebbles and fossil-wood are in the scrub and on the melon-hole flats.

"February 23rd.—I moved on to the water-holes, which I had found the day before, and encamped in the shade of a *Fusanus*. The latitude was observed to be 22°6′53″ . . . . . At about a mile-and-a-half from the camp, a large creek, apparently from the southward, joined the river, and water was found [February 24th] in a scrub creek four miles from the camp; also in wells made by the natives in the bed of the river; and, at about eight miles from the camp, we came upon some fine water-holes along the scrub. Here the birds were very numerous and various: large flights of the blue-mountain and crimson-winged parrots were seen; Mr. Gilbert observed the female of the Regent-bird, and several other interesting birds, which made him regret to leave this spot so favourable to his pursuit. He returned, however, to bring forward our camp to the place, whilst I continued my ride, accompanied by Brown. Several creeks joined the river, but water was nowhere to be found. The high grass was old and dry, or else so entirely burnt as not to leave the slightest sign of vegetation. For several miles the whole forest was singed by a fire which had swept through it; and the whole country looked hopelessly wretched. . . . . Towards sunset we heard to our great joy the noisy jabbering of natives, which promised the neighbourhood of water. I dismounted and cooeed; they answered; but when they saw me, they took such of their things as they could and crossed to the opposite side of the river in great hurry and confusion. . . . Their camp was in the bed of the river, amongst some small Casuarinas. Their numerous tracks, however, soon led me to two wells, surrounded by high reeds, where we quenched our thirst. My horse was very much frightened by the great number of hornets buzzing about the water. After filling our calabash we returned to the camp of the natives, and examined the things which they had left behind; we found a shield, four calabashes, of which I took two, leaving in their place a bright penny for payment; there were also a small water-tight basket containing acacia-gum; some unravelled fibrous bark, used for straining honey; a fire-stick, neatly tied up in tea-tree bark; a kangaroo net; and two tomahawks, one of stone, and a smaller one of iron,* made apparently of the head of a hammer: a proof that they had had some communication with the sea-coast. The natives had disappeared. The thunder was pealing above us, and a

---

* Sixteen years later A. C. Gregory made a similar observation amongst the aborignes, who so far had had no known communication with Europeans.

rush of wind surprised us before we were half-a-mile from the camp, and we had barely time to throw our blanket over some sticks and creep under it, when the rain came down in torrents. The storm came from the west; another was visible in the east; and lightning seemed to be everywhere. When the rain ceased we contrived to make a fire and boil a pot of tea, and warmed up a mess of gelatine soup. At eight o'clock the moon rose, and, as the weather had cleared, I decided upon returning to the camp, in order to hasten over this dreary country while the rain-water lasted. The frogs were most lustily croaking in the water-holes which I had passed, a few hours before, perfectly dry, and never were their hoarse voices more pleasing to me. But the thunderstorm had been so very partial, that scarcely a drop had fallen at a distance of three miles.* This is another instance of the singularly partial distribution of water, which I had before noticed at Comet Creek. We arrived at the camp about one o'clock a.m.; and, in the morning of the 25th February, I led my party to the water-holes, which a kind Providence seemed to have filled for the purpose of helping us over that thirsty and dreary land. Our bullocks suffered severely from the heat; our fat-meat melted; our fat-bags poured out their contents; and everything seemed to dissolve under the influence of a powerful sun.

"The weather in this region may be thus described: at sunrise some clouds collect in the east, but clear off during the first hours of the morning, with northerly, north-easterly, and easterly breezes; between ten and three o'clock the most scorching heat prevails, interrupted only by occasional puffs of cool air; about two o'clock p.m. heavy clouds form in all directions, increase in volume, unite in dark masses in the east and west, and, about five o'clock in the afternoon, the thunderstorm bursts; the gust of wind is very violent, and the rain sometimes slight, and at other times tremendous, but of short duration; and at nine o'clock the whole sky is clear again. In the hollows along the Isaacs, we found a new species of grass from six to eight feet high, forming large tufts, in appearance like the oat-grass *(Anthistiria)* of the Liverpool plains and Darling Downs; it has very long brown twisted beards, but is easily distinguished from *Anthistiria* by its simple ear; its young stem is very sweet, and much relished both by horses and cattle. . . . . . The bed of the Isaacs was overgrown with reeds and full of pebbles of concretions of limestone, and curious trunks of fossil trees; and on its banks a loose sandstone cropped out. Here [February 26th] we found the skull of a native: the first time that we had seen the remains of a human body during our journey. Near the scrub, and probably in old camping-places of the natives, we frequently saw the bones of kangaroos and emus. . . . I found a shrubby, prickly *Goodenia*, about four or five feet high, growing on the borders of the scrub. . . . On February 27th the natives had, in my absence, visited my companions, and behaved very quietly, making them presents of emu feathers, bommerangs and waddies. Mr. Phillips gave them a medal of the coronation of Her Majesty Queen Victoria, which they seemed to prize very highly. They were fine, stout, well-made people, and most of them young; but a few old women, with white circles painted on their faces, kept in the background. They were much struck with the white skins of my companions, and repeatedly patted them in admiration. Their replies to inquiries respecting water were not understood; but they seemed very anxious to induce us to go down the river. . . . On February 29th we started and travelled about ten miles in a north-east direction, leaving the

* E. Favenc in his pamphlet, *The Great Austral Plain*, calls attention to this curious partial rainfall.

windings of the river to the left. The character of the country continued the same; the same ironbark forest, with here and there some remarkably pretty spots; and the same Bastard-box flats, with belts of scrub approaching the river. At about nine miles from Skull Creek, which I supposed to be in latitude 21°42′, the Isaacs breaks through a long range of sandstone hills; beyond which the country opens into plains with detached patches of scrub and downs, with "devil-devil" land and its peculiar vegetation, and into very open forest. The river divides into two branches, one coming from the eastward, and the other from the northward."

At Skull Creek the party were detained from the 1st to the 4th March, owing to an attack of lumbago from which Leichhardt was suffering. When he started out he notices that "Basalt cropped out on the Plains; the slight ridges of devil-devil land are covered with quartz pebbles, and the hills and bed of the river are of sandstone formation. A yellow and pink *Hibiscus* were frequent along the river." His calculations gave Skull Creek long. 148°56 and lat. 21°42 approximatively. Continuing up the Isaacs he notes "The Corypha Palm is frequent under the range; the Ebenaceous Tree, with compound primate leaves and unequilateral leaflets, is of a middle size, about thirty feet high, with a shady and rather spreading crown. We travelled about seventy miles along the Isaacs. If we consider the extent of its Bastard Box and narrow-leaved Ironbark flats, and the silver-leaved Ironbark ridges on its left bank, and the fine open country between the two ranges through which it breaks, we shall not probably find a country better adapted for pastoral pursuits .... March 7th, I moved my camp through the mountain gorge [through which the Isaacs breaks], the passage of which was rather difficult, in consequence of large boulders of sandstone and of thickets of narrow-leaved Tea-trees growing in the bed of the river. To the northward it opens into fine gentle Ironbark slopes and ridges, which form the heads of the Isaacs. They seem to be the favourite haunts of emus; for three broods of them were seen, of ten, thirteen and even sixteen birds. About four miles from the gorge, we came to the heads of another creek, which I called Suttor Creek after — Suttor, Esq.,* who had made me a present of four bullocks when I started on this expedition; four or five miles further down we found it well supplied with fine water-holes .... The Marjoram was abundant, particularly near the scrubs, and filled the air with a most exquisite odour."

Leichhardt was now following down the Suttor to the north-west and leaving the Mackay district. He was popularly said to have been a poor "bushman" and to have been without proper control of his men, and there is probably a great deal of truth in this statement.† But on the other hand this young Prussian was, for those times, well prepared scientifically for his work. He was a painstaking and accurate observer, full of enthusiasm and accomplished a bold and magnificent piece of exploration which will stand to his credit for all time.

In the following year, 1846, Wide Bay was surveyed by the Government Surveyor Burnett, who discovered what is now known as the Burnett River, and this discovery led to the opening up of the district by the squatters in 1847, headed by James Reid. Burnett brought back with him a castaway native of Tahiti, known as Geo. Moir, who had been living with the blacks. The year 1847 witnessed the

---

* This man was probably a partner in the then well-known firm of Suttor, Mocatta and Lee, of Bathurst.

† *See* Hy. Stuart Russell.

first attempt to form a settlement at Port Curtis. Lord Stanley had arranged to form a penal settlement there, but Mr. Gladstone succeeding him at the Colonial Office had the scheme carried out, and hence the name of the settlement came to be known as Gladstone.* The "Lord Auckland" carrying the new Governor and his party, entered Port Curtis on 25th February, 1847, and struck on a shoal, a bad omen to begin with, and on the 9th May following the "Thomas Lowry" landed the majority of the party back in Sydney. Some settlers remained, squatters amongst whom may be mentioned the Hay brothers who brought cattle overland, and so the process of settlement kept expanding northward.

---

* *See* Hogan's work previously referred to. Port Curtis had been surveyed by Surveyor General John Oxley, in November 1823, in H.M. Cutter "The Mermaid."

Fig. 6.—View of "Scrub" at the Alexandra Plantation, Port Mackay, from a photograph taken in 1866. The large trees are the Silk Cotton Tree (*Bombax Ciba*), with great buttress roots from which the Aborigines used to make their shields. These buttresses are seldom more than 2 inches to 3 inches thick without the bark, and are the nearest approach to a natural plank. The trees grow up to 80 and 100 feet in height. The palms seen on the left are of two distinct varieties the *Seaforthia elegans*, and the Alexandra palm, similar in general appearance; but the ends of the fronds of one are pointed, and in the other ragged as if torn by the wind, but they are not so torn, but natural.

CHAPTER III.

EXPLORATION ON COAST AND INLAND, 1847—1859.

On the 3rd December, 1847, H.M.S. "Rattlesnake," a twenty-eight gun ship, under the command of Capt. Owen Stanley, anchored under No. 2 Percy Islands and encountered rough weather there. On board was McGillivray the botanist. Three years previously, in 1844, he had been collecting further north for Lord Stanley above referred to (afterwards Lord Derby), and had joined the "Bramble' when she went up the coast in that year. He thus describes this island when he visited it in the "Rattlesnake."

"This is the largest of the Percy Isles, being about twelve or fourteen miles in circumference. In structure, it may be said to consist of a series of hills running in ridges: many of them covered with Gum-tree scrub; and all with long grass growing in tufts, concealing the loose stones, and rendering walking very laborious. On the western side of the island, about a mile from the anchorage, the sea communicates, by a narrow entrance, with a large basin, partially blocked up with mangroves, among which a creek filled at high water, runs up for a mile. At the head of this hollow a deeply worn dried-up water-course indicated the periodical abundance of fresh water; and by tracing it up about a mile further, I found many large pools among the rocks containing a sufficient supply for the ship, but unavailable to us in consequence of the difficulty in getting at it. Signs of natives were frequently met with, but none were recent. From the quantities of turtle bones about the fire places, it is evident that these animals occasionally resort to a small sandy beach near the entrance of the basin above alluded to.

"The botany of the island afforded at this unfavourable season not more than five or six species of plants in flower, some of which I had met with elsewhere. A species of Pine, *Araucaria Cunninghami*, is found here in small quantities, but more plentifully on the adjacent Pine Islets, where it appears to constitute the only arboreal vegetation. A few Cabbage palms, *Corypha Australis*, are the only other trees worth mentioning. Among the birds observed, black and white cockatoos, swamp pheasants, and crows were the most numerous. A fine banded snail, *Helix Incei*, was the only land-shell met with. A *Littorina* and a *Nerita* occur abundantly on the trunks and stems of the mangroves, and the creek swarmed with sting-rays *(Trygon)*, and numbers of a dull green swimming crab.

"During our stay the bush was thoughtlessly set on fire by some of our people, and continued burning for several days, until nearly the whole island had been passed over; the long, dry grass and dead trees blazing very fiercely under the influence of a high wind. At night the sight of the burning scrub was very fine when viewed from a distance, but I did not forget that I had one day been much closer to it than was pleasant—in fact, it was only by first soaking my clothes in a pool among the rocks, emptying the contents of my powder flask to prevent the risk of being blown up, and then making a desperate rush through a belt of burning scrub, that I succeeded in reaching a place of safety." On the 7th December the vessel passed through Whitsunday Passage but did not proceed more than sixty miles beyond Cape Upstart, whence she returned to Moreton Bay. On returning through Whitsunday Passage "a small bark canoe with two natives came off to within a quarter of a mile of the ship, shouting loudly and making gestures to attract attention," but the "Rattlesnake" being short of water could not stop.

"On the 29th April, 1848, the "Rattlesnake" left Sydney in company with the barque "Tam o' Shanter," Captain Merionberg, which carried to its destination the ill-fated Kennedy expedition. When the news of the disaster, which had overtaken Kennedy and his party, reached the settled districts, the vessels "Freak" and "Harbinger," Captain Simpson, with the faithful aborignal, Jacky*, on board, were sent up the coast to make further search. On the 15th April, 1849, shortly after rounding the north end of the North Percy Islands, Jacky pointed out from the "Freak" two white men on the island, who were making signals. When taken off by one of the boats they represented themselves as shipwrecked seamen, cast away in the schooner named the "Buona Vista," from Port Nicholson, bound to Torres Straits for Beche de Mer. One of the men, named Clarke, after much hesitation, admitted they had another companion whom he thought must be dead; he was found about a hundred yards from where Captain Simpson's party landed, insensible, and remained so till sunset, when he died : the two men were taken to the "Freak." Their story and conflicting statements excited suspicion. It was reported next morning that Clarke had been tearing up papers and throwing them overboard. Captain Simpson picked up some of the scraps, on one of which was an address to 'Mathew Clarke, on board the "Marion," Woolwich,' and sufficient to prove their story false, and he had no doubt that they were runaway convicts. This conclusion seemed to be further established on an after examination of what was found on the island, on which they buried the body of the dead man, a purple mark on whose throat, coupled with the prevarication of the two survivors, raised a strong suspicion of foul play.

In the meanwhile the activity on the coast was more than equalled by the exploration and settlement inland. The township of Maryborough was established on 2nd February, 1851, and on January 1st, 1853, the first Government Resident was appointed to Moreton Bay ; and two events were shortly to occur which gave a fresh stimulas, if such were needed, to the ever northward flowing tide of European immigration. The one was the Archers' Settlement, on the Fitzroy River ; and the other was the rush to the Canoona Goldfield. On the 10th August, 1855, the Archer party arrived at the station they named Gracemere on the Fitzroy River. This party consisted of Charles Archer, in command, Thomas Archer, H. W. Risien, second in command, Charles Beeman, various Europeans, natives, cattle, horses, etc. They had come up from the Burnett. On the 1st September their boat, the "Elida," came up with supplies, in charge of Colin Archer and one sailor. This was the first navigation of the Fitzroy, and the first cargo (Wool) from this river left on the 28th December, 1855, in the "Albion," Captain Hardy, which had arrived on the 15th of that month. In September of that year, the Messrs. Elliott had come up with their

---

* When H.M.S. "Pioneer" was examining Rockingham Bay, Mr. Walter Hill, the Government Botanist, found on the 29th September, 1862, on the banks of the Mackay (Tully) River a new species of Banana, which he named *Musa Jackeyi*, in honour of this faithful Australian.

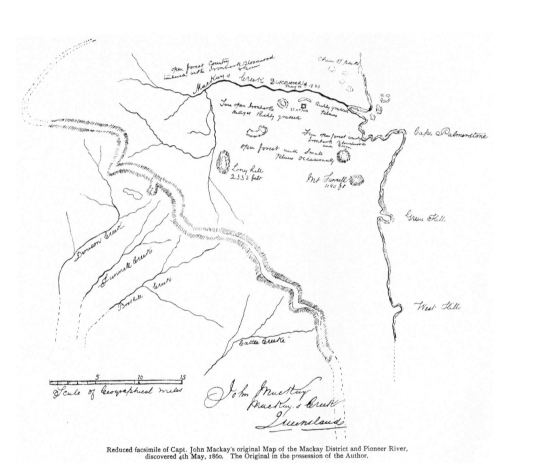

Reduced facsimile of Capt. John Mackay's original Map of the Mackay District and Pioneer River, discovered 4th May, 1860. The Original in the possession of the Author.

To accompany *Port Mackay, Queensland,* by H. Ling Roth, 1908.

stock, but did not start Canoona Station until March, 1856. The success of the Archers naturally drew others to this part of Queensland, amongst them, that much, and unjustly, maligned man, Wm. Landsborough. He was the son of a Scotch medical man, was born in Ayrshire, and educated at Irvine.* He started as a Squatter in New England, and like many others explored on his own account: and thus it was that in 1856 he discovered and named Nebo and Fort Cooper. In the meanwhile A. C. Gregory was returning from the Gulf Country in search of Leichhardt, getting into the back country of Mackay, but a long way inland. He camped on the Burdekin on the 29th October, 1856, and viewed the junction of the Burdekin and Suttor Rivers the following day; for several days after this he was. in touch with the Suttor. On the 3rd November he notes " The marks of iron tomahawks are frequent where the blacks have been cutting honey or opossums out of the hollow branches of the trees," showing how the white men's tools were indicating their proximate advent. On the 5th November, having now passed the

latitude of Sir Thos. Mitchell's last camp on the Belyando, and thus connected his route with that of Dr. Leichhardt, he considered it unnecessary to follow the river further, and decided on taking a south-easterly route to Peak Downs and the Mackenzie River. On the 10th November he was approaching the watershed of the Fitzroy River, and hoped soon to emerge " from the vast tract of scrub which occupies the valley of the Suttor River. On the plain we observed that more than half the Box trees had died within the last three years, and that they had not been killed by bush fires, as the old timber which lay on the ground was not scorched." On the 15th November he was on the Mackenzie River, and on the 17th he crossed the Comet River and here found traces of one of Leichhardt's Second Expedition Camps. On the 22nd November he writes :—" At 8 o'clock came to a dray track, which was followed east-north-east two miles to Messrs. Conner and Fitz't Stations, where we met a most hospitable reception." This was at Rio Station, on the Dawson River. Dan Conner soon after this moved northward and took up Marlborough, Princhester and Willangie Stations, as well as Collaroy. Henning purchased Marlborough from him, and Van Wesen purchased and formed Princhester.

Fig. 7.—Dan Conner. He and his partner, H. B. Fitz, welcomed A. C. Gregory on the Dawson in 1856. He was the second to ship wool from Gladstone and from the Fitroy River. He was forming Collaroy Station in July, 1860, when Mackay passed through on his return from the discovery of the Pioneer River. He was amongst the first to build a house (Lansdowne) at Port Mackay, and was afterwards made Excise Officer and Inspector of Distilleries at Mackay. Conners Range, Conners Crossing and Conners Creek are all named after him.

Willangie was sold by Conner to Wm., Aug., and Geo. Hurst (Hurst Bros.), who were stepsons of Fitz. Willangie was afterwards owned by Mark Christian. Conner writes me about this as follows :—" I was in partnership with Mr. H. B. Fitz,

* Was Landsborough one of the Landsborough Bros. who took up sheep land at Monduran, Burnett River, about 1847?

† Henry Bates Fitz was the owner af Pilton Station, Darling Downs. Four years later he was made a member of the Legislative Council of Queensland.

not on the Suttor, but Rio Station, Dawson River, purchased from Haughton Bros., but the sale was never completed. I stocked it sometime in 1853, being the outside Station then north, the only occupied run near me was Rannes, 30 miles south, owned by the Hay Bros. Rio was the first Station made [*i.e.,* arrived at] by A. C. and Henry Gregory—his brother, on their Expedition across, from the head of the Gulf Country to Brisbane. They stayed with me a few days and then pushed on to Rannes. Conner River and Range were both named after me ;* also Conner's Hump —the latter by A. Macartney, of Waverley—while we were out upon an exploring trip to look at that country. It was on this occasion he named a point on the Range by the name in question ; he purchased the Station and shortly after stocked it—this was after I had formed Collaroy, in 1859."

The progress of settlement had now touched upon the Mackay District, and received a fresh impetus by the discovery of gold in 1858 by a man named Chapple, on Canoona Station, which had been sold by "Hobbey" Elliott to Ramsey & Gaden, who in turn had sold to Vicary. Of the thousands who were disappointed with these diggings a few remained to colonise this part of the country, and as a matter of fact these diggers who remained behind were the makers of Rockhampton. On October 8th of this year, Rockhampton was made a Port of Entry; on the 17th October, the first Rockhampton land sales were held at Sydney, and on the 15th December, 1860, the town was proclaimed a Municipality.

But some fourteen months before this, on 16th October, 1859, Captain H. Sinclair and James Gordon made the valuable discovery of a port which they named Bowen or Port Denison. They had started from Rockhampton on the 1st September, in the "Santa Barbara," met with rough weather and were five days repairing on No. 2 Percy Island. On the 25th they anchored to the westward of the largest of the Cumberlands, and on the evening of the 27th they anchored on the western side of Middle Island, in Edgecumbe Bay, and after considerable labour made the discovery. Sinclair had been induced to start on this voyage by a proclamation of the Government of New South Wales offering a large reward for the discovery of a port north of Port Curtis; but on the 9th December of that year, 1859, Queensland was proclaimed an independent Colony. New South Wales said Queensland must pay the reward, but Queensland said it had made no promise ; so between the two governments Sinclair went unrewarded, a fate which afterwards befell Captain Mackay. It is extraordinary that the settlement of this splendid natural port has not made greater progress than it has done; it should, before now, have been one of the chief towns in the north of Queensland, but the success of Townsville, in the north, and the success of Port Mackay, in the south, drew away the few go ahead residents it once possessed, and it has not yet recovered this loss.

In August, 1860, the "Spitfire" was despatched by the Governor, Sir Geo. Bowen, to examine the coast, under the command of J. W. Smith ; G. E. Dalrymple,† Mr. Stone, surveyor, and Mr. Fitzallan, botanist, accompanying him. The vessel "passed through the group of Northumberland Islands, which are described as of a most pleasing appearance. Their summits rise to 600 or 800 feet, and were clothed

---

* It is a curious fact that although Dan Conner spells his name with an 'e' (Conn*e*r and *not* Connor), all the Queensland maps spell the name *erroneously* 'Connor.'

† Geo. Elphinstone Dalrymple (brother of Sir Jas. Elphinstone Dalrymple, Bart., M.P. for Portsmouth, England), did a considerable amount of exploration, and became afterwards M.L.A. and Colonial Secretary.

with Acacias, Gum Trees, Cyprus, Laurel, and groups of very beautiful and useful Pine. The adjacent Pine Islands of Capt. King, formed unbroken forests of straight Pines of large dimensions, and afforded an excellent harbour. These islands are visited by Natives of the neighbouring continent but are not permanently inhabited." In due course the " Spitfire " visited Port Denison and reported thereon.

Of the Percy Islands G. E. Dalrymple writes :—" On the 5th September, 1860, we anchored in the harbour formed by No. 1, 2 and 6 Percy Islands, and close under the first-named, off Beale's Creek watering place. The Percy Islands appear to be formed of a coarse sandy conglomerate which forms the cliffs and headlands of their coasts, and crops out on the crests of the hills. Grassy hills rise to an elevation about 800 feet, openly timbered with Eucalypti, Casuarinae, Pandanus Palms, &c., the valleys and richer flats are densely wooded with fine pines of the *Gums Cookei* and small belts of scrub, in which are Bottle Trees, Yellow Wood, Acacias, Iron Wood, and a variety and network of Scrub Vines and Creepers. These Islands are well adapted for cattle pastures, while portions of considerable extent are suitable for cultivation. The Botanical Collector attached to the Expedition here obtained specimens of a new and very beautiful terrestial orchid *Vauda Ceruliensis*. Mr. Hill, Director of the Botanical Gardens at Brisbane, first discovered this beautiful plant on No. 2 Percy, in 1854; but the attack of the aborigines, which resulted in the murder of his companion, Mr. Strange, obliged him to abandon his specimens. .... Mr. Smith completed observations at the former observatory spot of H.M.S. " Herald," where we found a post bearing the inscriptions ' H.M.S. HERALD, CAPT. DENHAM, R.N., JULY, 1859.' Having filled up with water from the clear running stream of Beale's Creek, on the 6th of September we stood away W. by N., passing No. 2 Percy, Sphynx, and Pine Islands, &c. Smokes from fires kindled by the blacks rose from the hills of the former. The " Spitfire " passed the high peak of Prudhoe Island at 9-0 p.m., and during the night and following morning, the others of this group. At 10-0 a.m. of the 7th September, L Island rose three miles off on our port beam. These Islands are lofty. some clothed with stunted dark green timber to the hill tops ; the last-named sweeping upwards in beautiful grassy slopes from a rocky shore to a more peak shaped summit ; deep ravines furrow its sides, clothed with dense dark scrub. At 2-0 p.m. we ran along under the precipitous sides of M Island, which rises sheer out of the sea in crags and grassy and thickly wooded steeps of *Eucalypti, Fici*, Pines, &c., to an elevation of 874 feet.

"Dense clouds of smoke rose from the fires of the natives on the W. side of the island. . . . . . Blacks were seen on the beach carrying their canoes up out of the water into the thickets. They then ascended the hills, and saluted us with wild cries as we proceeded to our anchorage. We landed in the whale-boat on the western island, the natives awaiting our approach on the beach, but taking again to the hills when we neared the shore. Some very neat bark canoes were found close to the beach, and another was seen paddled by a native at the opposite side of the harbour. They are formed of three sheets of bark taken from a Eucalyptus ; are about 8 feet long, 3½ feet broad, and 20 inches deep ; are pointed and turned up at both ends, and are very neatly and strongly sewn together with a long, tough, cane-like creeper. Two cross sticks between the gunwhales keep the whole in form. In each canoe was a very neatly made paddle, ornamented with cross of red paint, or raddle, on the blade. Several large shells to hold water or bail out, a piece of *Vauda Ceruliensis* of about 6 inches long (purpose unknown), a long coil of fishing line, very neatly made, probably of the film of the *Pandanus Palm Leaf*, and to which was attached a spear head of about 5 inches in length, neatly barbed and pointed with a very hard and sharp fish bone. These spear heads are fitted into a socket in the end of a long spear, which the blacks throw from their canoes with considerable precision into dugong, turtle, or other large fish. The barbed point remains in the flesh, the spear floats off and is picked up; the line, fast to the spear head, is then paid out, and the fish is run and killed, very much as whalers capture their more gigantic prey. From the appearance of a dugong found newly killed in a camp on Upstart Bay, it would appear that the canoe is kept close over the fish, which, on rising to the surface to blow, is assailed with waddies and spears, there being no less than 13 broken spear points in the head and shoulders, the snout and forehead being also considerably disfigured by the blows of Nullah Nullahs (native clubs)."*

The result of all the discoveries, was that *while the country surrounding what is now known as the "Mackay District," had become more or less known and was being rapidly settled, the district itself was as yet not dreamt of.* It seems anomalous that to the north, south and west the country should have been settled, and the coast fairly well explored, while the comparatively small district lying in the centre had not yet been seen by a European. The explanation probably lies in the fact that, from Mount Funnell, the mountainous range trends more or less north-west away from the coast, and, with its thickly timbered country, not being considered suitable for sheep stations, deflected the direction of settlement, which, with a different surface configuration, would have progressed in a more northerly direction. But the discovery of the district was imminent, and had best be told in the words of Captain John Mackay, the leader of the party which discovered it.

* At Cape Cleveland he writes :—"the canoe taken from the natives to prevent co-operation from the mainland, was quite different from the others along the coast, being formed of one large sheet of bark about 10 feet long, sewed up at either end with the same cane-like creeper used for this purpose all down the coast, and was capable of carrying 6 or 7 men. The paddle was of different and more rude construction than those further south, and the natives themselves taller, very black, and of a more savage cast and expression of features. I have remarked that the aborigines about M. island take out the right front tooth; those on Mount Dryander the left, while those seen in Cleveland and Halifax Bays have no such peculiarity at all." (Report of the Proceedings of the Queensland Government Schooner, "Spitfire," in search of the mouth of the River Burdekin, Brisbane, T. P. Pugh, 1860).

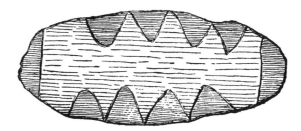

Fig. 8.—Native Mackay Shield, in Bankfield Museum, Halifax.

CHAPTER IV.

CAPTAIN MACKAY'S EXPEDITION.

Captain John Mackay's Narrative* of the Discovery is as follows :—" The year 1859 found me, like hundreds of my profession, trying my luck as a digger on the Rocky River Goldfields, N.S.W. Having, in time, made the acquaintance of some young men whose relations owned station properties in the district, a trip to the far north in search of country for their rapidly increasing flocks and herds, was often discussed in my tent, and always concluded with a pressing invitation for me to join them, holding out as an allurement an immense fortune to be acquired as a squatter. The rainy season coming on and my claim all but worked out, I at last acquiesced with their wishes, in which resolve, however, I fear a love of adventure proved the strongest incentive. After a few days preparation, we left Armidale on the 16th January, 1860, the party consisting of Messrs. John Macrossan, H. Robinson, A. Murray, John Muldoon, D. Cameron, John Barber, myself, and Duke, an intelligent aboriginal black boy, and splendid horseman. We had 28 horses with the usual outfit, pack-saddles, fire-arms, etc. As a description of our journey to Rockhampton would, I fear, prove of little interest, I will merely state that we travelled via Tenterfield, Warwick, and across the Darling Downs to Gayndah, thence to Glad-

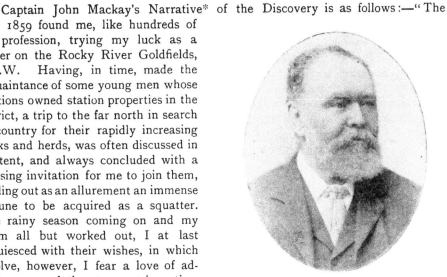

Fig. 9.—Capt. John Mackay, the discoverer of Port Mackay. He was born 26th March, 1839, at Inverness, Scotland, and received his education at the Free Church Academy in that town. He first came to Queensland in the ship "Australia," Capt. Mowbray Mountain, arriving in Melbourne in 1854 ; coming to Sydney in the following year in the sister ship, "South Carolina," Capt. Chas. Leisk. While on the Rocky River diggings, in 1859, he was chosen leader of the Expedition which discovered the Pioneer River. Financially, the expedition was a failure and John Mackay returned to his early love, the sea, and for nearly twenty years was a well known and much respected commander of various vessels in the South Sea and New Zealand trades. He was appointed Harbour Master of Cooktown in 1883, and afterwards transferred to the higher post at Brisbane.

stone by the Kolan and Boyne Rivers, arriving at Rockhampton on the 2nd March.

* This and many other notes were given me by Captain Mackay when he visited Port Mackay, in 1882, for the first time since his departure in 1863 ; others were given me by him when I was his guest during his subsequent harbourmastership in Cooktown, and others, together wlth a printed pamphlet, published at Singleton, N. S. Wales, in 1892, entitled *Discovery of the Pioneer River*, he sent me on my return to England.

Here we camped with the view of refreshing our horses and completing final preparations—repairing and altering pack-saddles, jerking beef, and other endless jobs conducive to the success of the journey. Our party* was also reduced by Messrs. Cameron† and Muldoon,‡ the former returning to New South Wales, and the latter going into business at Rockhampton.

"On the 16th March, being all in readiness, we left Rockhampton, proceeding towards Yaamba. Our horses proving very restive, we were greatly retarded by some of them bolting throughout the day, resulting in the loss of several useful articles. We had on starting 5 cwt. flour, 6 cwt. jerked beef, 20 lbs. tea, 100 lbs. sugar, 20 lbs. coffee, some corn flour, groats, and sundry medicines; each man carried 5 lb. powder, 100 bullets, 8 lb. shot, 4 boxes caps, a double-barrelled fowling piece, and Colt's navy sized revolver. We had two ordinary compasses (one fitted on saddle bow), a prismatic compass, sextant, artificial horizon, a map of Queensland recently published, a general chart of Australia showing coast line, and Leichardt's track from Moreton Bay to Port Essington, with a copy of the Journal of his First Expedition. We had 28 horses, each man being provided with two riding hacks, the others used solely for packing. Camped on the river about 15 miles from Yaamba; we were greatly annoyed with mosquitoes during the night.

"The following day passed Yaamba, and camped near Princhester.

"March 18th.—Late start in consequence of horses having strayed, passed Princhester,§ proceeding in company with a party of Victorians bound west (Peak Downs). Camped together at a muddy water-hole; sleep, owing to the ferocity of sandflies and mosquitoes, was all but impossible.

"March 19th.—Started early, still travelling in company, arriving at Marlborough at 8 p.m., where Mr. Henning was forming a station. Here we remained until the 22nd., the country in the direction in which our course lay being reported very boggy, and all but impassable. All hands repairing pack-saddles, etc.

"March 22nd.—Left Marlborough and bade farewell to civilisation, proceeding in a westerly direction towards the range, dividing the waters of Broadsound and the Isaacs River. Towards evening the country became more broken, consisting of stony ironbark ridges, well grassed. At sundown we camped on a creek running to the S.W., and while preparing supper were surprised by about a dozen of the natives, well armed, appearing on the opposite side of the creek, and, fearing others might be

---

* John Macrossan born in County Tyrone, Ireland, came to Australia in 1840, and was a store-keeper at Uralla. Hamilton Robinson was born in Singleton, N.S. Wales, in 1838, where his father was Superintendant of the Rothbury Estate of Messrs. R. and H. Scott, of Glendon. A. Murray was born at Bendemere, N.S.W., about 1838. John Muldoon was born in the North of Ireland, came to Australia in 1854, and was goldmining at Uralla. D. Cameron was a native of Furness, in Scotland, and came to Australia in 1851; he was manager of The Retreat Station, in New England. John Barber (*not* Barker) was an Italian ship's carpenter, whose correct name was Giovanni Barberi, but for short he was called John Barber; he came to Australia in 1858.

† Cameron was never heard of again. He left a wife to whom he had only been married two years.

‡ Muldoon went into partnership with a grazier named Mackenzie, and was drowned in the Fitzroy in 1866.

§ Mr. Van Wesen's.

in the vicinity, Robinson fired over their heads, when they fled down the creek. A good watch was kept during the night.

" March 23rd.—Started about 8 a.m. and began to ascend the range, which here was steep and broken. About noon we gained the top, from which a splendid view of the surrounding country was obtained. To the westward, the valley of the Isaacs River presenting one immense scrub, stretched to a line of peaks in the distance, the heavy timber with darker foilage indicating the serpentine course of the river, along which the smoke of several blacks' fires could be observed. To the N.N.E., the waters of Broadsound and Shoalwater Bay were distinctly visible, till away in the distance sea and sky were blended together. At 3 p.m. we began to descend the western side of the range, over stony but well grassed ridges, moderately timbered with stunted Ironbark and Bloodwood. At sundown we camped on a deep creek running to the westward, in which Duke and myself suceeeded in catching some fish of the bream species. Night cool.

" March 24th.—To-day we travelled in a westerly direction, with the view of striking the river; we were considerably retarded by occasional patches of dense brigalow scrub, some of which we managed to get through in single-file, but often had to deviate from our course to avoid them. About noon a large party of natives crossed ahead of us on a small plain, when having gained the edge of the scrub, they sent the women and children away, remaining themselves, with the apparent intention of stopping our further progress. Rounding the pack-horses up, Macrossan, Duke and I went towards them, when one of them, suddenly darting out on the plain, hurled a spear in the direction in which Duke was approaching, which fortunately fell short of the mark. We at once fired over their heads, when they disappeared in the scrub, leaving their war implements and a net containing some fish and a large iguana.* Taking the fish we left in payment a tomahawk, a sheath knife and a pumpkin. Camped on the Isaacs River, which here was a deep, broad stream, with immense Ti-trees lining the banks.

" March 25th.—To-day we began our northward journey along the valley of the river, a recital of which would prove but of little interest, each days' experience being so similar in incident, such as cutting our way through dense scrub, swimming creeks, etc. At times the monotony would be broken by a party of natives, usually returning from a fishing or hunting excursion to camp. We occasionally shot a scrub turkey and some ducks, but we were unable to get within shot of a kangaroo, though plenty were observed each day as we went along.

" On the 1st of April we arrived at the junction with the river of a large sandy creek, from the N.E., in latitude 22°10 S. which, although differing from the position assigned to it on the map; I supposed, to be Denison Creek.

" 1860, April 2nd.—To-day we continued along the river to the westward, over box flats, and brigalow scrubs; at 5 p.m. came to the junction of another creek, from the northward, which I believe to be the main stream of the Isaacs, though Leichardt on his journey appears to have followed the western, and what he considered the principal branch. At sundown we crossed to the western bank and camped.

" April 3rd.—Proceeded to-day in a N.N.E. direction, the country becoming more ridgy and covered with stunted Ironbark and Bloodwood. At noon the latitude by Mer. Alt. was 21°40 min. S. longitude, by dead reckoning 148°33 E. At 4 p.m.

---

* There are of course no *Iguanas* in Australia; the reptile referred to is a species of *Agamidæ*.

could observe a range ahead, extending from N.N.E. to N.W. with two remarkable looking peaks close together. Camped on a small lagoon, where Barber and Robinson succeeded in shooting some ducks.

"April 4th.—Started early, travelling over broken and stony ridges well grassed. At noon arrived at the foot of the range seen on the day previous, and making for a gap bearing about N.E., passed over without difficulty, and camped at sundown on a creek flowing to the N.N.W., supposed by us to be a tributary of the Suttor of Leichardt.

"April 5th.—Started early, and in a N.W. direction along the creek, over well grassed ridges moderately timbered with a kind of Box, Bloodwood, and occasional clumps of brigalow scrub. At noon arrived at the junction of another considerable sized creek from the S.E. below which it assumed a good size with both high banks, and plenty of water. At sundown prepared to camp on the east bank, but while unsaddling our horses we heard the cooeys of the natives as if following our tracks in pursuit. We proceeded on our way until midnight, when, coming to a large water-hole in the bend of the creek, we tied the pack horses up, and keeping watch in turns, lay down to sleep.

"April 6th.—Travelled to-day more to the westward, along the creek, which for size might be designated a river, the country becoming more level and scrubby than on the previous day. At 11 a.m. we arrived at where another creek of equal size joined it from the southward, the junction of which was in latitude 20° 50 min. S., and in longitude D.R. 147° 45 min. E., which places us considerably to the east of the Suttor River of Leichhardt, and the position assigned to it on the chart, on which no river is shown flowing north, between the Suttor and the coast. From the junction it flowed a considerably sized river with a good supply of water, and trending more to the northward. In the afternoon observed the letter D and broad arrow cut in a Bloodwood tree, the bark having been stripped and the figures cut deep. About two miles further on, came to where several trees bore the same mark, and the site where a tent had been pitched, which we concluded must be Dalrymple* and party, who left Rockhampton some three months before our arrival. As I believed this to be undoubtedly a tributary of the Burdekin, we continued on our course, and at sundown camped between a lagoon and the river, where Murray and I shot some ducks. Night very cold.

"April 7th.—Started early and travelled in a N.N.W. direction on the west bank of the river, over well grassed flats and low ridges timbered with Ironbark, Bloodwood and Box. During the day observed several small creeks join the main stream from the eastward, and several marked trees as on the day previous, travelled till late, and camped on the river.

"April 8th.—Travelled as on previous day along the river, which now flowed in a N.N.W. direction, the country being flat, and apparently subject to inundation, latitude at noon 20° 20 min. S. At 2 p.m. we suddenly came on a party of natives, apparently one family, comprising an old man, a gin and three picaninnies. On us approaching them the old man fled, leaving his better half and offspring to do the best they could. On our alighting they sat down in the long grass, and seemed greatly terrified, the mother hugging her young ones with fond affection. Macrossan gave her some cotton and needles, showing her the use of them, and then attired her

---

* The official referred to on p. 26.

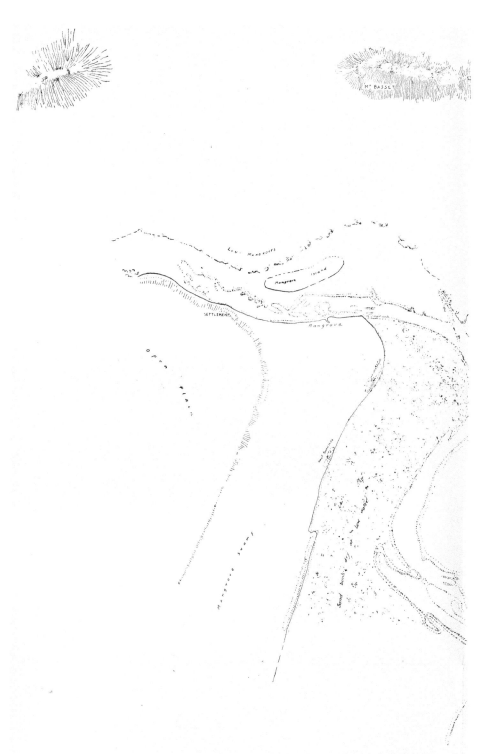

To accompany *Port Mackay, Que*

NOTE: For the sake of clearness in the reduction the soundings shewn in the original
cause or result of the southern deflection of the mouth of the river, was broken through in the grea
in their channel instead of allowing them to spread, a strong scour was established in flood
broken through.

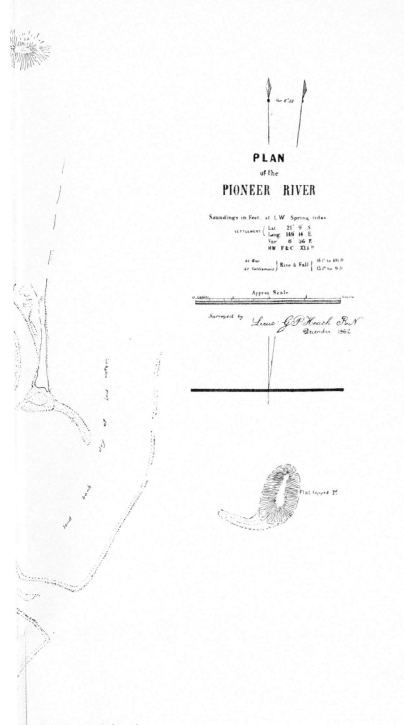

PLAN

of the

PIONEER RIVER

Soundings in Feet, at L W Spring tides

SETTLEMENT
Lat 21° 9' S
Long 149 14 E
Var 6 56 E
HW F&C XI h

At Bar
At Settlement } Rise & Fall {
16 ft to 10 ft
13 ft to 9 ft

Approx Scale

Surveyed by *Lieut G P Heath R N*
December 1862

Flat topped I^d

Round I^d

...l have all been omitted.   The long, sandy spit with the broad end, which was the original
...at storm of 1898.   With the erection of the training walls, which kept the waters of the river
...l times which was accentuated by the heavy rainfall of the storm mentioned, and the spit was

in a white shirt. We made signs to her for water as if wanting a drink. She at once pointed towards the river, exclaiming ' Bianee, anee! Bianee anee!'. They seemed highly pleased at seeing us depart, and I have no doubt but the terrified husband would be agreeably surprised to see his better half returning to camp arrayed in the under garment of a white man! Camped at sundown on the river; night very cold.

"April 9th.—Were rather late in starting, some of the horses having strayed. Proceeded as on the day previous in a N.W. direction, over alternate flats and clumps of scrub; at 11 a.m. arrived at the junction of another large river from the southward, which we had no doubt was the Burdekin. It was here fully a quarter of a mile broad, with high banks, between which was nothing but an immense sand-bed, with thickets of Ti-tree at intervals with only a small stream of water meandering in its sandy bed. Were greatly disappointed at its appearance, and small supply of water. The latitude of this camp (approximate) Mer. Alt. Aldebaran, was 20° 47 min. S.

"April 10th.—As it was apparent from the several marked trees, that Dalrymple and party had taken up the country, not only along the river, but also the tributaries,* after a brief consultation, we agreed to retrace our steps south, and strike more to the eastward than on our outward journey. On the general chart in our possession there appeared an immense area of *terra incognita*, between the Burdekin and the watershed of the Isaacs River, extending eastward to the coast, on which was noticed by Leichhardt ' heads of a large river supposed to flow into Repulse Bay.' Travelled until 8 p.m. and camped on a small creek, where we remained until the 14th washing and mending clothes, cleaning firearms, etc.

"From this date to May 12th a portion of our journal is missing, and the remains so obliterated as to make it quite unintelligible. So far as memory serves me we experienced no incident worthy of note, and camped often in consequence of wet weather.

"May 12th.—Started early in an easterly direction with the view of striking the river we had followed coming north (which I may mention is the Bowen). At 4 p.m. we came to a lagoon, and fearing we might be unable to find water further on we camped. Macrossan shot some ducks, and Duke killed an immense iguana. Night cold with frost.

"May 13th.—Started early in an E.S.E. direction, and 3 p.m. struck our out-ward trail, thence along the creek to the S.E. At 4 p.m. came to where some white men had camped a few days previous, showing that another party had gone north, which we avoid meeting by not following the river. Camped on a creek coming from the S.E. Latitude from Mer. Alt. Regulas, 20° 37 min.

"May 14th.—Started early, proceeding as on the day previous over flats and low ridges covered with stunted Ironbark and Bloodwood. Observed several kangaroos, which were too shy to get within shot of them. In the afternoon the country became more broken and stony, indicating our approach to the range. We had crossed more to the westward on our outward track. Camped on a small muddy water-hole, with just sufficient water for ourselves and horses.

"May 15th.—Proceeded as on day previous across steep and broken ridges. Latitude noon, 21° 14 min., long. D.R. 148° 22 min. E. In the afternoon proceeded in a more easterly direction along a well watered creek, coming from the eastward,

* See Dalrymple's reported itinary below.

5

at the head of which we camped in a weird looking spot, surrounded by broken and precipitous mountains.   Night very cold with heavy frost.

"May 16th.—Remained in camp with the view of refreshing the horses, and discovering an available gap over the range to the eastward.   After breakfast, accompanied by Macrossan and Duke, I ascended a high mountain near the camp, from the top of which we had a fine view of the surrounding country.   Looking coastwise we observed an immense tract of level country ; unbroken save by an occasional hill or peak, extending away in one expanse to the sea-coast.   To the north there appeared a practical gap, the ridges nowhere abrupt.   Close to the camp Duke killed a carpet snake fifteen feet long.

"May 17th.—I started at sunrise, and proceeded in an E.N.E. direction toward the pass we had seen the day before, which we found much steeper than we anticipated, and the surface being loose stones, the travelling harassed the horses very much.   At 2 p.m. we gained the dividing water-shed and commenced our descent on the eastern side of the range.   Finding no water at sundown, and being moonlight, we proceeded on our way, and at 10 p.m. came on to a large stony creek, with a good supply of water, running to the eastward where we camped.

"May 18th.—Started early along the creek which was very rough and broken. At noon we came to where it was joined by a large creek from the southward, from which junction it flowed in a northerly direction, a bold deep river, with well defined banks, which in places were rendered quite picturesque with clumps of palms and other tropical vegetation, unlike anything we had previously seen.   Mr. Macrossan proposed that our discovery should be named the Mackay River, to which the others agreeably assented.   Observed for the first time several alligators, firing at some, but without effect.   At sundown crossed the river and camped on the eastern bank.

"May 19th.—Proceeded on our way along the river, passing occasional clumps of thick tropical scrub, in which we found a delicious fruit, of a reddish colour, and resembling an English cherry.   At 3 p.m. came to where a considerable creek from the N.W. joined the river, which now flowed in an easterly direction.   Camped at the junction.

"May 19th. [*sic*]—Started early, proceeding along the river to the eastward, over flat forest country timbered with Ironbark and Bloodwood, with occasional clumps of large Ti-tree.   In places travelling was rendered slow and difficult owing to the country being full of holes, and mounds of stiff black soil.   In the evening Murray shot a kangaroo which enabled us to spare our supply of meat, now considerably reduced.   Latitude at noon, 21° 8 min. S., longitude by D.R. 149° E., which, if near the truth, places us within twenty miles from the ocean, and nearly in the latitude of where two islets are marked on the coast.   Camped on the river ; night very cold.

"May 20th.—Proceeded along the river as on day previous.   At 10 a.m. came on to a plain extending from the river back to a chain of low grass hills to the southward.   Travelling slow through the long grass, the black soil full of holes and mounds resembling mole hills.*   At 4 p.m. came on to a chain of water-holes,† which appeared to form a semi-circle with the river, enclosing a splendid tract of country, richly grassed.   At sundown we made for the river, where its aspect showed that we were approaching the ocean.   Mangroves now appeared on the banks, and on tasting the water found it brackish.   Having no fresh water, we were obliged, tired and jaded, to retrace our steps in the dark to a water-hole we had passed in the afternoon,

* Commonly called " devil-devil."   † Now known as The Lagoons, Mackay.

when each man on unsaddling his horse went to sleep in the long grass, oblivious of any danger there might be moving round us. Towards morning we awoke with drizzling rain, making things very uncomfortable.

" May 21st.—Packed up at sunrise, and without breakfast, proceeded along the river to the westward, in search of a favorable spot to camp, which we found where a precipitous ridge jutted into the river, its inaccessability leaving nothing to fear from that side, while the background was clear and open. Here we turned the horses out and pitched our tent. While Murray and I were cutting a track through a clump of scrub to the fresh water, I observed a milky juice exude from the cut branch resembling cocoanut milk, we both partook of some and found it rich and agreeable, but which injudicious act we suffered for afterwards, our tongues and mouths becoming blistered and swollen to such an extent, that partaking of food or drink for some days afterwards was a painful operation. Heard the cooeys of the natives close to during the day. Watch kept.

" May 22nd.—All hands washing and patching, cleaning firearms, etc. Robinson and Duke complained of severe headaches, and were unable to partake of any food. Succeeded in shooting some ducks, and Macrossan shot a scrub turkey, the broth of which Robinson and Duke slightly partook. Night extremely cold.

" May 23rd.—The sick men being no better, and supposing it to be the primary symptoms of fever and ague, small doses of quinine were administered night and morning. Accompanied by Barber and Macrossan, I proceeded at 9 a.m. to the coast in order to observe the latitude of the mouth of the river, but having to cut through dense scrub, it was 3 p.m. when we reached the beach at a sandy point forming the south side of the entrance, and from which I observed that the north bank overlapped the entrance in a long sandy point. Returning to the camp, we observed some blacks well armed with spears, but on approaching they fled towards the river. Sick men no better. Night cold.

" May 24th.—Accompanied by Murray and Macrossan I started early to the mouth, where at noon I made the latitude by a Mer. Alt. to be 21° 10 min. S., which nearly corresponds with our latitude by account, as from the direction it flowed, from where we discovered it, I supposed it to flow into the sea at Slade Point. Returning to camp I cut the letter M on several trees along the river, this portion having fallen to my lot when drawing for the respective blocks of country to be taken up. Duke and Robinson still unwell.

" May 25th.—Duke slightly improved but Robinson worse, and Murray complaining. Macrossan and Barber discovered another creek about five miles south, and running parallel with the Mackay. Shot a turkey close to the camp, the broth of which seemed to improve the sick men. Night very cold.

" May 26th.—Were rather alarmed this morning by observing several blacks' fires close to camp. As the two sick men were showing no signs of improvement, we packed up, and started back along the river, Macrossan and I marking trees on both sides as we went along, and crossing at intervals for that purpose. At 4 p.m. Murray and Robinson became so ill that we were obliged to camp. Night fine and clear, but very cold.

" May 27th.—A week had now elapsed since sickness made its appearance in the camp, but this morning all, excepting Macrossan and myself, complained more or less of severe headache, and pain in the back. Murray and Robinson were unable to dress, or mount their horses. About noon we managed to pack up, and proceeded along the river, camping at the junction of the creek from the N.W.   Being moonlight Macrossan and I marked some trees on the opposite side of the river, being the portions alloted to Murray and Robinson.   Night very cold.

"May 28th.—Remained in camp, my sick comrades much worse.   Some of the horses having strayed to our previous camp.   Macrossan and I started in search, leaving the firearms within easy reach of the sick men, to enable them to make some little resistance, should the blacks appear in our absence.   Finding the horses about five miles from camp, we retraced our steps, but when ascending the river bank near a clump of scrub, we were suddenly confronted by five sable warriors with clubs, and the largest spears I had seen.   As they apparently intended to impede our further progress, my gun being charged with shot, I fired low, aiming at the legs of the ringleader, when they at once disappeared leaving their war implements, and two large fish behind them.

"May 29th.—This morning Macrossan was on the sick list, but his brave heart and generous nature, reluctant to give in, he still kept knocking about.   The others so ill as to render a start impossible.   In the afternoon the smoke of several fires was observed on the opposite bank.   But since sickness made its appearance in the camp, watching regulations became lax, indeed all but impossible, so that an attack by blacks was viewed as a secondary danger.   This with the scanty supply of provisions left, about 50 lbs. flour (sour), 4 lbs. sugar, 20 lbs. insipid jerked beef, and some tea.   On the whole, our proceedings now partook of a gloomy and desponding aspect, the hilarity that characterised our outward journey gradually taking flight.   Night cold with drizzling rain.

"May 30th.—Remained in camp, Macrossan better, the others not improved. In the forenoon went in search of something fresh to make broth for the sick.   A lagoon close by swarmed with ducks, but being extensive, and no trees along the margin, it was impossible to get within shot of them.   In the afternoon we caught some small fish, which the sick men partook of.   Here we remained until the 7th of June, obtaining each day a scanty supply of fish, which appeared to improve Robinson, though no change in the others.   Murray suggested killing one of his horses, but having no salt, and the weather too cold to preserve it by jerking, we dissuaded him from it, as we could only utilise a day's supply.

"June 7th.—Robinson and Barber slightly better.   We managed by 10 a.m. to pack up and start along the river to the southward.   I managed to shoot a small kangaroo, and Macrossan a scrub turkey, so that, for a few days at least, our larder was well supplied.   Being fine moonlight we intended travelling all night, but at 10 p.m. Murray and Duke were unable to ride any further.   Unpacked, but fearing the horses might stray to our last camp we tied them up, Macrossan and I keeping an alternate watch.   At daybreak I shot two opposums, which proved a welcome addition to our stock.

"June 8th.—Murray and Robinson slightly improved, the others no better. Got a start at 9 a.m., Macrossan riding Barber's horse, while Robinson and Murray alternately supported Duke, myself following the pack horses, who, as if instinctively conscious of our forlorn and helpless condition, proceeded quietly along in single file, giving no trouble.   We now began to ascend the range dividing the waters of the Mackay* and Isaacs Rivers.   The thoughts of being homeward bound appeared to

---

* The Mackay River, now of course known as the Pioneer River.

cheer and exhilarate my sick comrades very much. Travelled till sundown, when, coming to a stony creek running to the eastward, we camped, keeping two of the horses tied up, fearing the others would stray. Night very cold.

"June 9th.—Barber and Duke being too weak to ride, we remained here until the 13th, shooting a number of brownish colored birds, a species of pheasant, the broth of which greatly improved the sick. We also caught a number of crayfish, of which Duke heartily partook. Nights very cold with sharp frosts.

"June 13th.—All the sick slightly improved. We managed to get away at 10 a.m., at noon we began to descend the southern side of the range, and after sundown came on to a large sandy creek, in the head of which was revealed by the bright moon, a small silver stream threading its serpentine course noiselessly along. Shortly after midnight Duke fell from his horse, I at once raised him up, but appearing faint and exhausted we stopped the horse to allow him a rest, and lighting a fire, boiled some of the flour, which, sweetened with sugar, Macrossan, Robinson, and myself heartily partook of. At 3 a.m. all ready to continue our journey, I went to raise Duke up and assist him to mount, but to my surprise and sorrow I found that the stream of life had ebbed, and poor Duke was no more. We at once unpacked the horses and turned them out. Then making the sick as comfortable as possible, Macrossan and I, in the grey dawn of morning, dug a grave in the loose sand bank, and wrapping poor Duke in his coat and blanket, laid him down in his last resting place. Although of a different race, the poor fellow's death was keenly felt by all, for no more faithful companion could man have than poor Duke. Knowing him from childhood, Macrossan was, if possible, more grieved than the others, and his sudden demise tended to considerably augment the despondency already prevalent in the camp. Here we remained until the 19th June, endeavouring to resuscitate the sick of various kinds. Murray and Barber, declaring they could proceed no further, implored us to proceed and leave them to their fate."

Here I may digress from my journal to remark that it has been my lot since then to participate, more than once, in some of the dire events that tend to make the seaman's life a chapter of thrilling adventure. But the few days succeeding Duke's death stands out through the long vista of years in a bolder and more harrowing relief than any other incident of an eventful life. We knew that each day's delay lessened the chances of the sick, or even ourselves, reaching civilization, so far as we knew, 150 miles distant. But, determined to stand by them to the last, we looked forward with stolid indifference to whatever Fate might have in store for us. Each morning accompanied by my brave comrade (Macrossan) we wended our way to the creek in silence where on catching a few small fish, one of us would return and broiling them on the coals, give to our sick comrades to partake of, then returning to the creek for another supply. And so on, day by day.

"June 20th.—Murray and Barber were to-day so far recovered as to be able to walk without any assistance, I was also fortunate enough, when searching one of the saddle bags for percussion caps, to find a pot of Liebig's essence of meat, and the tea of which, with the simple fish diet, so easy of digestion, I attribute the safety of their lives. On the 26th I shot an immense iguana, which, though to me the most repulsive of reptiles, was skinned and consigned to the pot, the sick partaking heartily, with ourselves, of both soup and meat.

"June 29th.—To-day the sick men were so far recovered as to enable us to get a start at 11 a.m. Macrossan leading Murray's horse, proceeding in a southerly direction along the creek, travelling till late and camped on the west bank. Night very cold.

"June 30th.—This morning I was pleased to observe a marked improvement in all hands. Murray and Robinson assisting to pack up, Barber still weak. Travelled S.S.E. along a broad sandy creek, which in my opinion is the most important tributary of the Isaacs. At noon we were agreeably surprised to meet three white men, who for a supply of food were as bad off as ourselves. They were Mr. Andrew Scott, of Hornet Bank, Dawson River, a Mr. Ross, and Mr. William Fraser, whose family had been murdered by the blacks some years previously. We at once agreed to travel in company, and make common stock of our respective scanty supplies, proceeding to Rockhampton. Towards sundown I felt the first symptoms of fever, in the shape of an intense headache, followed by such a severe fit of the shakes as to make riding a difficult matter. We camped on a small plain surrounded by scrub, and there being no water, tied our horses up. The horrors of that night I shall never forget, the fever producing a burning thirst; and our evening meal having exhausted our supply of water I was unable to quench it. During the night a heavy dew had fallen, and while the others were packing up I crawled, more than walked, to a small gully, which, following for about 100 yards in the scrub, I found about a pint of muddy water, which, from the dead leaves, had a strong, pungent taste—to me it was nectar.

"July 1st.—Travelled to-day through scrub, and alternate plains, crossing occasionally a small chain of water-holes. During the day I felt better, though still very weak. From Mr. Scott I learned that since our departure from Rockhampton several stations had been formed in Broadsound and on the Lower Isaacs. The night being fine and clear we continued our way south, along a broad sandy creek, until arriving at midnight where another joined it from the N.W. we camped at the junction, when the last of our flour and sugar was used to make supper for all hands. As we observed during the day that the country was infested by blacks, on Mr. Scott's suggestion, a good watch was kept.

"July 2nd.—Started early, having breakfasted on the last of our jerked beef. At noon I was again attacked with fever, but managed to ride along. Having crossed the creek of yesterday to the eastward, we travelled in a southerly direction through open forest country, with occasional clumps of dense brigalow scrub. At sundown we arrived at a broad sandy creek or river which, on crossing, we were pleased to observe the tracks of drays and trail of a herd of cattle which ran along until midnight, when we arrived, hungry and jaded, at where Mr. Conner was then forming Collaroy Station, where we remained until the 5th, refreshing ourselves and horses.

"July 5th.—Started early across the Broadsound Range, arriving at sundown on the low land, where we camped with Mr. John Allingham, then travelling with stock in search of country.

"July 6th.—Proceeded on our way south, passing the camp of Mr. Macartney, at Waverley, and arrived at 8 p.m. at Marlborough, after an absence of nearly four months. The following day proceeded to Rockhampton, arriving on the 8th, when, disposing of our horses, and tendering, in accordance with Crown Lands Regulations for the respective runs taken up, sailed for Brisbane on the 19th July, in the s.s. "Tamar," commanded by the genial Captain Cotter. Returning to Armidale my journal was published in the *Armidale Express and Maitland Mercury*.⁎ We then tendered for the country we had taken up, in accordance with the Crown Lands Regulations, which tenders were at first rejected, in consequence of the river, which we had named the Mackay, and the locality being unknown.

⁎ On his return Macrossan retired from his business, built a flour mill, and died wealthy in 1881. Barber returned to Uralla, where in 1866 he was accidentally killed by the falling of a tree, the cutting down of which he was superintending. Murray became the owner of Bannockburn Station, and made money at the tin mines. Hamilton Robinson became a farmer and grazier at Manilla, some 40 miles distant from Tamworth, and at Glendonbrook, where he settled down ; he married in 1864.

Fig. 10.—Tramway on the " River " Estate in 1880. Percy Crees (nephew of John Spiller and manager) stands on front of the engine, in a line with the funnel, and Bob Walker (manager of " Foulden ") is squatting on the bogie on the right.

Fig. 11.—View of Mount Spencer, the house and lake. The Hon. Henry S Finch-Hatton (now Earl of Winchilsea and Nottingham) with gun and Basil Brooke in the boat. From a photograph, by G. H. M. King (Fryerne), taken in 1883.

CHAPTER V.

LOCAL EVENTS WHICH FOLLOWED CAPT. MACKAY'S DISCOVERY.

Early in 1861 the tenders for the respective runs claimed for by Mackay's party were accepted by the Queensland Government, from which date they were allowed nine months for stocking the same, failing which any persons putting stock on could legally claim the country. " In order " says Mackay " that I should (if possible) derive some benefit from the adventure, on Mr. Macrossan's recommendation I entered into partnership with a then well-known squatter, Mr. James Starr, of Mihi Creek, on the apparently equitable conditions, that while he furnished so many cattle I should find the country, each one contributing to the incidental expenses of forming the station, taking cattle overland, etc. Un- fortunately for both of us my partner was then already in difficulties, his property being mortgaged to the firm of Jas. Dickson & Co., Merchants, Sydney. In pursuance of the agreement I left Armidale on the 26th day of July, 1861, with 1,200 head of cattle, 50 horses, and two teams of bullocks. The party consisted, besides myself, of four stockmen, two bullock-drivers, carpenter, cook, with Jerry and Jimmy, two intelligent blackboys, hailing from the Macleay River, N.S.W. I travelled via Tenterfield, Warwick and Dalby, thence on to the Burnett River, which, following to the head, I crossed the range on to the watershed of the Dawson River. Passing Camboon, owned and managed by a large hearted Scotch- man (Mr. Reid), I passed Banana, Rannes, and Westwood, arriving at Rockhampton on 27th of October. Our stores having arrived from Sydney, I left our camp outside Rockhampton on the 9th November, and crossing the Fitzroy at Yaamba, travelled via Princhester and Marlborough. Then passing through the Broadsound country, where several stations were then forming, I arrived at the foot of the coast range on November 17th. Here we had to doublebank the teams, dividing the loads into portions of half a ton each, which, even thus reduced, getting one load on the top, a distance of slightly over a mile, was considered a good day's work. On the evening of the 20th, I succeeded in getting drays and stores on top, and crossing the cattle the following morning, proceeded along a well beaten track towards the Isaacs River, by which that prince of bushmen, Mr. Nat Buchanan and others had travelled to Fort Cooper, where a camp was then made.

" On the 2nd December I arrived at Denison Creek, which I consider the most important branch of the Isaacs, and travelled along it ; our progress being retarded by the loose, deep sand, making it difficult for the teams to keep pace with the cattle.

" On the 10th December we camped near the spot where we had buried Duke, more than twelve months before. What a change had taken place—even in that short time ! The natural stillness that hitherto pervaded the forest, was then unbroken save by the cooee of the sable nomad of the soil. Now, the lowing of

6

cattle and crack of the stockman's whip, were all significant of the march of civili-sation, and presaging to the hitherto dark rulers of the soil, that the enemies of their race were too surely approaching. We crossed the range in a north-easterly direction from Denison Creek, and not where the Nebo Road now [1882] crosses the range. The traveller of to-day can hardly realise what we had to encounter, getting drays, stores, etc., down the steep creek sides and ravines at the head of Bell and Sutherland Creeks (now Stockyard and Blackwaterhole Creeks), and the constant watch necessary to guard against attacks from the blacks, who were both numerous and hostile.

" On, I think, the 26th of February, 1862, I succeeded in getting the two bullock teams and drays to the lagoon at the foot of Greenmount Hill, where I afterwards built a hut and stockyard and where myself and party, consisting of four

Fig. 12.—Greenmount. The Cattle Station formed by
Capt. John Mackay.

whites and two blacks, resided for more than five months in ignorance of what was taking place in the outer world. We were living chiefly on fresh meat and milk —flour, salt, tea and sugar had long since given out in consequence of the non-arrival of the vessel I had arranged for with my agent at Rockhampton, Mr. Mansfield.

" In June, 1862, I was agreeably surprised by a visit from Mr. Geo. Elphinstone Dalrymple, Commissioner for Crown Lands for the Kennedy District, who, accom-panied by some native troopers, was now on his way from Port Denison, his quarters, to Broad Sound, along the coast. Dalrymple had arrived at Port Denison on March 10th, 1862, after proving that the Wickham River was the real outlet of the Burdekin River. He remained with me three days, visiting the sea coast, where at the mouth of the river he verified my former latitude 21° 10 S. He also named the two remarkable looking hills on the north side of the river Mounts Blackwood and Jukes, in honour of the commander and naturalist of H.M.S. " Rattlesnake."

With one of my black boys I accompanied him as far as Mount Funnell, and, never having the pleasure of meeting him again, I may here remark that the few days visit of this intelligent gentleman remains with me as the most pleasant reminiscence of my sojourn at Mackay.

" Having now concluded that some unforeseen contingency had interfered with the arrival of the vessel with stores, and our supply of that panacea for all troubles —'tobacco'—being now exhausted, I, with Jerry, blackboy, started for Fort Cooper, where I concluded that Nat Buchanan would be forming a station. We, however, had not proceeded far when we were surprised by meeting a party of three horsemen, comprising Messrs. Barr, Sadleir and Pringle, who had followed the trail of our drays across the range from the head of the Isaacs, but whose presence at such a time, and at such a place, remains to this day a mystery. They, however, informed me that a cutter with my stores had been duly dispatched, but, failing to find the mouth of the river, she anchored in a creek near Slade Point ; here one of her crew and a passenger, Mr. Roberts, being killed by the blacks, she at once returned to Rockhampton.

" Started again for Fort Cooper, when, on the second day out from Greenmount, I was surprised to observe from the top of the range an encampment on the lagoon, at the head of Denison Creek, afterwards known as ' Spencer's,' with cattle browsing all around, which on reaching I had for the first time the pleasure of making the acquaintance of my future comrade, Honest Dick Spencer,* who under the impression that he was furthest out was astonished to find it otherwise. From him I heard the first of Prince Albert's death, and a confirmation of the cutter with stores having put back to Rockhampton, and the murder of one of her crew. But from letters subsequently received he was told that as the vessel was about to sail again for the Mackay, his stores would be sent by her, and I would probably be ignorant of the steps taken, it advised him to proceed to the coast, inform me and keep a lookout. The following morning, accompanied by our two blackboys, we started for Greenmount and from thence to the coast, keeping a lookout from one of the hills on the north side of the river. After a few days anxiously gazing to seaward and no sail appearing, we proceeded along the coast with the intention of going to Broadsound, in which we were greatly retarded and harassed by our horses getting constantly bogged in crossing the numerous mangrove creeks. With nothing to subsist on excepting jerked beef, now of the consistency of leather, and the want of proper rest consequent upon watching at night, on the fourth evening from the Mackay we camped on the south side of Cape Palmerston, tired, hungry, and jaded to such an extent that we lay down, quite regardless of the future or of the dangers which surrounded us.

" The following day we fortunately saw the cutter at anchor. Sending the black boys home to Greenmount with the horses, we both got on board the cutter, which was the " Presto," Capt. Hart, getting under weigh the following morning, we two days afterwards entered the river, landing our stores about 100 yards above where the bridge, erected in 1875, crosses the Pioneer at The Hermitage. Taking all the stores to Greenmount, I then accompanied Spencer in search of a better track across the range than the one I had come by. This, with the help of the black boy, Billy, we

---

* John Hardy, of Fassifern. and Alf. Delves Broughton, of Ipswich, were the first to bring cattle to The Retreat, now called Mount Spencer Station. Spencer was originally only in charge, afterwards buying it. Jack Birby assisted Spencer in bringing up the cattle.

succeeded in finding where the Nebo Road now crosses. After finishing a marked tree line on to the tableland, Spencer and his boy returned for his drays, and shortly afterwards succeeded in conveying his stores by that route to the station. Here I would digress again and accord to the memory of this generous man, and his party,* a tribute of kindly remembrance, asking for his name, with those of his men, Raynor and Ready, an honoured and foremost place in the annals of the early times of Mackay.†

"I detained the cutter at a daily charter of £8 per day, and measuring a base line on the island, succeeded by a series of cross bearings in making a tolerable sketch of the mouth of the river, which, with soundings, correct latitude and general features, I sent to the Crown Lands Office, Brisbane, as shewn in Buxton's Map of Queensland, in the following year, 1863.

Fig. 13.—John Cook, of Balnagowan.

"In consequence of Mr. Starr's insolvency now declared, and the expenses defrayed in forming Greenmount being ignored by the mortgagees, Jas. Dickson & Co., and in order to pay the expenses of the cutter, no doubt considerably augmented by the double trip and by my detaining her to survey the river, I had to sell to Mr. E. B. Cornish, uncle to the Messrs. Bridgman, the pastoral lease of that known as Cape Palmerston run, *i.e.*, from the east boundary of Greenmount to the sea-coast, for £300. This cheque, with more added, was paid by me to Mr. Mansfield in the presence of Mr. Cornish. Messrs. Bridgman & Kemmis were perfectly cognizant of the above facts.‡

"Having now to proceed to Sydney to protect my interest in Green Mount, I gave charge of the Station to a Mr. Vince.§

"After leaving Geenmount and on my way to Rockhampton I met, on Denison Creek, Mr. Lewis Gerald Ross|| in charge of some cattle belonging to Mr. John Cook,

---

* This was the party which first came down Mackay's track with bullock drays, made up as follows :—Richard Spencer, Wm. Cristison, Ben Reynolds, Curley Ross, Stuttering Jackson, Jack Willis, Bill Allen, Harry Payne, Black Billy (aboriginal), and James Ready in charge of the teams. In December, 1862, Ready took a team to Broadsound and was stuck up for seven weeks by floods.

† Spencer was afterwards charged with shooting a notorious bully, under circumstances of great provocation. On this occasion the Mackay people subscribed £300 for his defence. Ready remained in the district, and Raynor settled in Roma.

‡ It has been said that Captain Mackay sold this run to Kemmis—which is evidently a mistake, although it would appear that Kemmis brought the first cattle to the Cape Palmerston Station.

§ Vince had been storekeeper and overseer for Julian, at Princhester. He was said to have been accidently killed afterwards by Mackenzie, a dairyman, whom Vince supplied with cattle. One day Vince had come late in to dinner at Cooke's Hotel, having just given Mackenzie a young bull. After dinner they went into the Billiard Room, had a dispute over the game, when Mackenzie it is alleged, struck Vince who fell uttering : "You've done for me this time," and expired. His death was probably accelerated by disease of the heart from which he was known to be suffering. There was no enquiry. Mount Vince, west of Greenmount, was called after him.

|| Ross had a partner of the name of Muggleton, who had teams on the road. Muggleton came down the range via Stockyard Creek, and through Hamilton to the present site of Mackay.

on their way to Burdekin in search of an imaginary run sold to Mr. Cook by a person named Allingham, but being short of provisions and the cattle very poor, he was very despondent as to his ultimate success. I then told him that the run taken up by me on the north side of the river, Shamrock Vale, now called Balnagowan, was as yet unstocked and was at his disposal. I hurriedly agreed with him as to its purchase for what he considered a fair value to be paid for after the run had been secured; pursuant to this I gave him all instructions by which he was enabled to take possession, thus forming the second station on the river. Before leaving Queensland, I visited Mackay with a view to a settlement. But 'no funds' an with Ross's subsequent early death, all my hopes of compensation ended.

"There were no houses at Mackay when I left but a Mr. Cridland from Fort Cooper and a Mr. A. Henderson* intended building. James Ready who came out with Spencer was the next to follow. So in reply to the often discussed question 'Who were the first to settle at the town of Mackay?' I have no hesitation in designating these gentlemen as the fathers of the hamlet. Mrs. Ready was the first white woman north of Broad Sound Range, and many of the old fever stricken pioneers since scattered far and wide must to the last retain grateful memories of her kind attentions while presiding at Spencer's Camp."

This ends Captain Mackay's narrative.

The river discovered was not destined to keep the name of its discoverer, for in 1862 Commodore Burnett visited the coast in H.M.S. "Pioneer,"† and as he had in honour of one of his officers named a stream flowing into Rockingham Bay the Mackay River,‡ he suggested that to prevent geographical mistakes, John Mackay's discovery should be named the Pioneer River in honour of that ship's visit to Queensland. The Government having no desire to detract from the merits of the discovery named the town, then being surveyed on its banks, 'Mackay.'

The news of Mackay's discovery seems to have taken some time to reach the public in the capital, for it was not until Friday, August the 15th, 1862, that anything about it was known. On that date the *Brisbane Courier* published the following statement :—

"DISCOVERY OF TWO NEW RIVERS TO THE NORTHWARD.

" Information was received yesterday from Rockhampton of the supposed discovery of a new river between Broad Sound and Port Denison, and that its geographical position is such as to lead to the belief that the discovery is one of great importance.

" The Collector of Customs has obligingly favoured us with a copy of the memorandum forwarded to him by the Officer of Customs at Rockhampton, and from it we gather the subjoined particulars.

" The river has been named the McKay, a gentleman of that name being the owner of a station some twelve miles up the stream. It is situated about five miles

---

* Henderson is said to have arrived before Cridland; he was afterwards the owner of the Beaconsfield Estate.

† When she went south in July. on the 10th of that month, her commander, Hugh Arthur Reilly, died, and Burnett took charge. He was in command of her when she made her second voyage up the coast between 27th August and middle of October. Burnett went down in H.M.S. "Orpheus" when she was wrecked on Manukau Bar, N.Z., 7th February, 1863, being the last of four brothers, all of whom were drowned at sea.

‡ Afterwards the name was changed to Tully River, after the Surveyor-General Alcock Tully.

south of Slate (or Slade) Point, and about thirty miles north of Cape Palmerston, and disembogues into a large bay not previously shown on the charts. It has the disadvantage of a bar entrance, open to the south east, but there is a channel a quarter of a mile wide over the bar, and a depth of sixteen feet of water upon it at high tide. The channel is, however, nearly dry at low water. The landing-place is about two miles from the bar, up the river, and fresh water is obtainable about three miles from thence. The banks are lined with the inevitable mangrove. At the landing-place the river is about a quarter of a mile wide, and at low water there is a kind of pool at the landing-place where there is about eight feet of water. The cutter " Presto " was the first craft to discharge cargo in the McKay, which she accomplished safely, and returned to Rockhampton. There is a good road to the landing-place from the stations in the neighbourhood, and there is every probability that a considerable shipment of wool will take place from the McKay during the coming season. The opening up of this river to navigation will also, it is stated, afford an outlet for the stations on the Isaacs river, Peak Downs, and other localities in that direction."

So far so good ; but now comes an extraordinary misstatement. The reporter continues :—

" We learn, upon further inquiry, that the McKay was discovered by Mr. Dalrymple, Commissioner of Crown Lands for the Kennedy district, on his outward journey to the Burdekin in 1859, and was followed down afterwards by Mr. McKay, an enterprising gentleman from Armidale, in New South Wales, to whom Mr. Dalrymple, on his return, had given a chart of his own route. Mr. McKay has now a very fine cattle station on its banks, near the sea, and here Mr. Dalrymple found him located on his late overland journey from Port Denison to Rockhampton. The McKay, Mr. Dalrymple informs us, is a swiftly running river, which takes its course through beautiful open forest country, affording excellent pasture for cattle. It discharges its waters into the sea, as previously stated, about thirty miles north of Cape Palmerston, but its mouth will only be available, Mr. Dalrymple thinks, for vessels of light draught of water.

" Another stream of some importance between Port Denison and Rockhampton is the O'Connell,* of which Mr. Dalrymple was also the discoverer, and which will yet be found useful for purposes of navigation. Its mouth was first seen by Mr. Dalrymple from the deck of the colonial sloop " Spitfire " in 1860,† and again, as late as March last, the same gentleman on his overland journey from Port Denison to Rockhampton, struck this river about two miles above its mouth. From the summit of a low hill, from which he obtained a good bird's eye view, he was enabled to follow its course, from its issue in the South Western Ranges, and thence winding through the low country to its point of embouchure in the southern end of Repulse Bay. Its mouth is quite as broad as that of the Brisbane, and Mr. Dalrymple believes, from the fact of their being rocky islands off the mouth, and from the absence of " break " that there is little or no obstruction in the shape of a bar. Mr. Dalrymple followed the river up for about fifteen miles before he could find a crossing place for his horses above the tideway, and he therefore believes the latter to be about twenty miles in length.

* Named after Sir Maurice O'Connell, President of the Legislative Council.

† When she was on her voyage to survey " Port Denison.

"Mr. Dalrymple states that he crossed magnificently rich country on the banks and side valleys of this river, better adapted for the cultivation of cotton, sugar, coffee, rice, tobacco, and other tropical productions than any coast land in Australia. The river, which he named the O'Connell, takes its rise from the high Fort Cooper Ranges, which form the watershed of the Isaacs, Bowen, O'Connell, and McKay Rivers. " We cannot close this notice of these important discoveries without expressing our obligations to Mr. Dalrymple for the courteous and obliging manner in which he replied to our enquiries. There could certainly be no better authority on all questions relating to the country between the Fitzroy and the Burdekin, and the information we have given may therefore be relied upon as perfectly correct."

It need hardly be said that the reporter completely misunderstood Dalrymple. According to Dalrymple's Journal of 1859 he travelled by the valley of the Isaacs on to the Belyando and Burdekin Rivers, tracing the latter to its embouchure, but not to the sea, and back to the Valley of Lagoons, and returned southward by nearly the same track. He went nowhere near the country traversed by Capt. Mackay. Moreover, had he known of the river discovered by Mackay some evidence of his knowledge would have appeared in the report of his subsequent voyage in the " Spitfire " in 1860. If any further evidence of the discovery made by Mackay should be required over and above that of the detailed account of Mackay and his associates—Hamilton Robinson confirmed it in 1892—we have Sir Arthur Palmer's certificate dated 1879. which reads as follows:—

" COLONIAL SECRETARY, QUEENSLAND.

To Mr. John Mackay,

    Master Barque " Meg Merrilies,"

        Auckland, New Zealand.

I hereby certify that the bearer, Mr. John Mackay, was known to me in 1860, when, as leader of an Expedition from New South Wales to Northern Queensland, he discovered (after a perilous journey of many months) the Mackay or Pioneer River with surrounding country, and subsequently became the founder of that port and town which now bears his name.

           (Signed) A. H. PALMER,

Brisbane, 8th September, 1879."   Colonial Secretary.

Fig 14—The first Alexandra Plantation House, erected by T. H. Fitzgerald.

PLAN OF THE TOWN IN 1866.

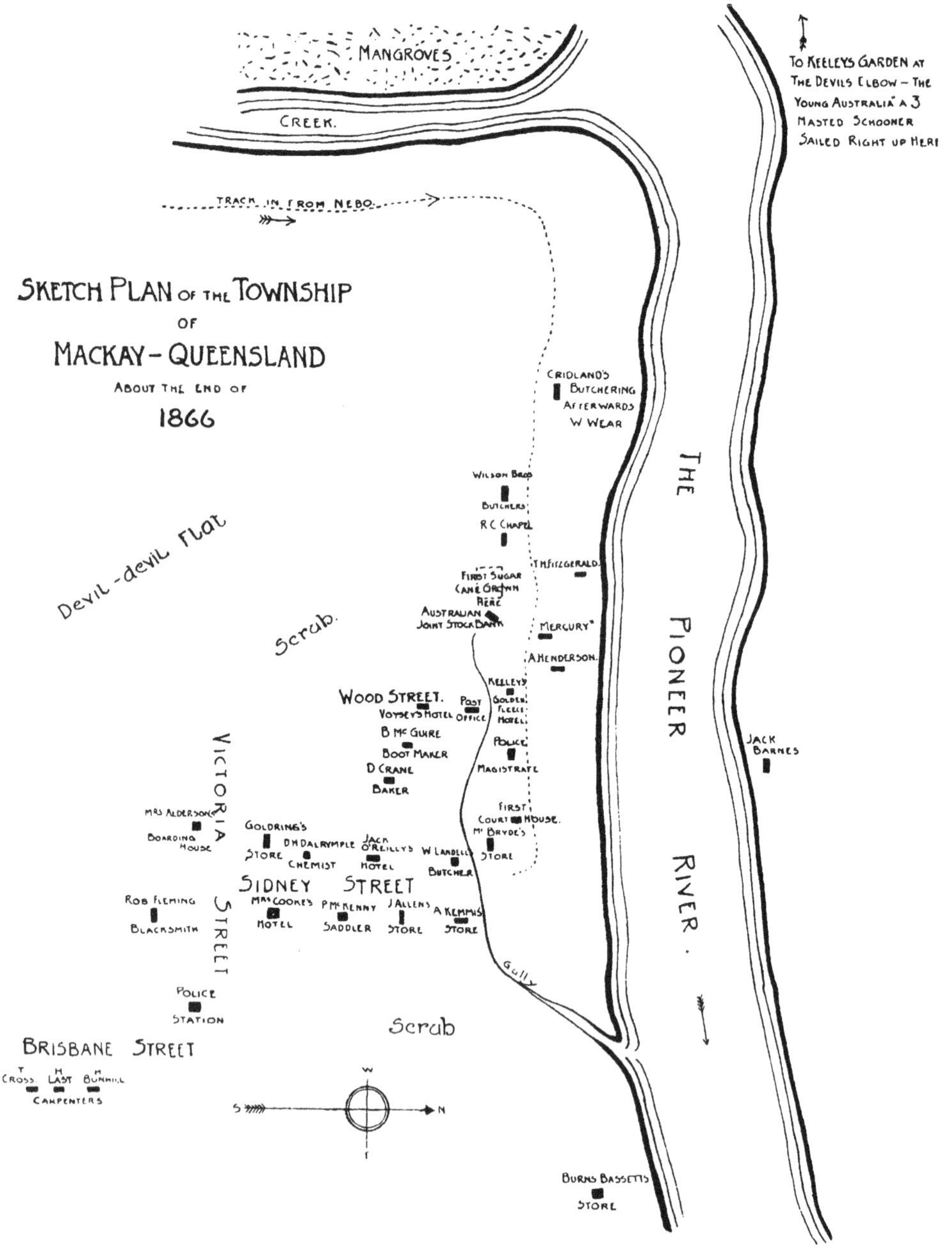

MANGROVES

CREEK.

TO KEELEYS GARDEN AT
THE DEVILS ELBOW — THE
YOUNG AUSTRALIA A 3
MASTED SCHOONER
SAILED RIGHT UP HERE

TRACK IN FROM NEBO

SKETCH PLAN OF THE TOWNSHIP
OF
MACKAY — QUEENSLAND
ABOUT THE END OF
1866

Devil - devil Flat

Scrub.

CRIDLAND'S
BUTCHERING
AFTERWARDS
W WEAR

WILSON BROS
BUTCHERS
R C CHAPEL

T H FITZGERALD.

FIRST SUGAR
CANE GROWN
HERE
AUSTRALIAN
JOINT STOCK BANK

MERCURY"

A HENDERSON.

WOOD STREET.
VOYSEY'S HOTEL
B McGUIRE
BOOT MAKER
D CRANE
BAKER

POST
OFFICE

KEELEYS
GOLDEN
FLEECE
HOTEL.

POLICE

MAGISTRATE

THE

PIONEER

RIVER.

JACK
BARNES

MRS ALDERSON'S
BOARDING
HOUSE

GOLDRING'S
STORE
D M DALRYMPLE
CHEMIST

JACK
O'REILLYS
HOTEL

W LAMBELL
STORE
BUTCHER

FIRST
COURT HOUSE.
Mr BRYDE'S

VICTORIA   STREET

SIDNEY   STREET

ROB FLEMING
BLACKSMITH

MRS COOKE'S
MOTEL

P McKENNY
SADDLER

J ALLEN'S
STORE

A KEMM'S
STORE

POLICE
STATION

BRISBANE   STREET

CROSS LAST BURRILL
CARPENTERS

Scrub

W

S   N

E

Gully

BURNS BASSETTS
STORE

Fig. 15.—The above Plan may be taken as a fairly accurate one at the period named. It is difficult at the present day to realise the wilderness of the site of the town as it was over forty years ago. Along the river (now River Street) was dense scrub and behind it that curious surface formation known as " Devil-devil " and Ti-tree swamps. On the spot where the first post office stood there was a scrub turkey's nest, and where Victoria Street now is the first settlers used to shoot wild ducks, etc. So late as when Keeley built the Golden Fleece he did it in thick scrub, and had to put up a notice on the river side track indicating the track leading to his hotel. Similarly, when Mrs. Cooke rented the hotel built by Henderson, at the corner of what are now Sydney and Victoria Streets, she had to cut a two foot track into the site of Victoria Street, which was then being made into a shorter cut from Nebo into town. It should perhaps be explained that when Mrs. Cooke moved lower down the street towards the river she took the name, Royal Hotel, with her, and the house she left being sold to K. H. Wills became known as Wills' Hotel. Voysey built the first two-storied building; it was afterwards occupied by Bill Lobie (Lobie and McCluskey, sawyers). After O'Reilly's death his house was kept by Philip Ilott until the A.J.S. Bank moved in. Capt. Hannah was in command of the " Young Australia " when she sailed up.

CHAPTER VI.

THE SETTLEMENT OF THE TOWN AND DISTRICT OF MACKAY TO 1866.

We must now hark back a little. When Mackay's party returned after their discovery of the river, they heard from Scott's party, as above mentioned, that settlement by squatters was quickly following on their heels, and in fact, when they arrived at one particular place they found it had been called Collaroy, and was being formed into a station by D. Conner. On 29th July, 1861, Landsborough and

Fig. 16.—"Lansdowne," the residence of D. Conner, mentioned by Lieut. Heath, R.N., when he surveyed the mouth of the river in 1862. Mr. and Mrs. Conner can be seen standing together near the nag's head. From a photograph taken about 1875.

Kemmis arrived at Fort Cooper. They had left Broadsound on the 24th June in company with Nat Buchanan, E. B. Cornish, and a black boy, parting at Peak Downs to look at some country 'discovered by Landsborough and Buchanan' some hundred miles or so beyond the Belyando. Landsborough then formed Fort Cooper. Cornish was said to have been a partner, and Kemmis was in full charge as manager; it was sold to Stewart and Lawson and later the cattle sent to Bowen Downs, and it was converted into a sheep station.* It is said that Nat Buchanan, having to abandon his cattle on the Belyando before reaching his destination, took some cattle from Fort Cooper early in the following year, 1862, and succeeded this time. In

* In 1867, when Kemmis was manager for Glen Walker & Co., he brought the sheep down to the rocks (Kemmis' Camp), the site of the Palms, and had them sheared there.

June, 1862, A. O. Brown arrived at Fort Cooper with sheep for Kemmis and Cornish, having left Sydney the year before and coming via Goonoo-goonoo station on the Peel river, in N. S. Wales; Brown is said to have brought the second mob of cattle over the range (from Fort Cooper) into the Mackay District to Palmerston run in 1863.

In the year 1862 Reynolds erected the first hotel at Nebo.   In May of this year a man named Irvine, who had come up with Till and landed where Barnes' garden was afterwards established, was killed by the Blacks while out looking for land; he is said to have had some cattle for taking up country with Murnin, Skinner and Anslow; Christian Langge was said to have been with him when he was killed, but managed to escape.   On the 23rd September, 1862, the s.s. "Murray" arrived at Mackay, she was the first steamer to come up the river and was intended to

Fig. 17.—Winterbourne. (G. N. Marten.)   Situated about a quarter of a mile west of Branscombe.   Dismantled about 1880.

ply between Rockhampton and Port Denison; she is said to have been originally a gentleman's yacht.   In the same month McKinlay, the explorer, passed through Fort Cooper on his way to Rockhampton, having arrived overland at Port Denison from Adelaide.   On October 2nd, Mackay was gazetted a Port of Entry no doubt on the strength of Captain Mackay's report, and on Nov. the 12th, the "Pancake" cutter arrived and landed stores at Lansdowne (D. Conner's) for the Retreat Station (Mount Spenser); her captain was known as Pancake Dick.

Ten days later, 23rd Nov., 1862, Lieut. G. P. Heath, R.N., arrived in the "Satellite," the Rockhampton Pilot Boat, and made the official survey of the river.   He reported " that any of the ordinary coasters of light draught which trade to the other ports in the Colony can enter the Mackay [Pioneer] river without any difficulty.   It is not however well suited for vessels of great length.   At the place where the vessels lie to load and discharge cargo there is about 5 or 6 feet at L.W. in a narrow channel" a second bank or bar about ¾-of-a-mile below the present settlement when nearly dry leaves this part of the river a perfectly sheltered basin where a vessel may, if her draught of water exceed 6 feet lie on the soft sandy bottom in perfect safety. The site of the present settlement is about four miles from the Bar. The bank abreast the anchorage is steep to, and about 18 inches above the level of H.W. spring tides. A very short wharf run off from the bank would enable vessels to lay in the channel to load and discharge; at present to effect this they lie alongside the bank and at low water ground on an incline which is objectionable. The bank here is evidently being fast washed away by the action of the stream, and should a township be laid out on this spot it will be necessary immediately to protect the bank above the site for the wharves from further abrasion.

Fig. 18.—The Nyth, near the Hollow. (E. S. Rawson.) Removed to The Hollow in 1881, where it was used as a Batchelors' Quarters, and burnt down in 1896. From a Photograph by E. S. Rawson.

" The river dries at low water about half a mile above the settlement and at a distance of one and a half miles a reef of rocks extends about two thirds of the way across the stream rendering the navigation somewhat dangerous for sailing vessels, and at a distance of three miles is another rocky barrier which effectually puts a stop to the further progress of vessels. In the neighbourhood of this latter spot it has been suggested to place the township, as there is an abundant supply of water in its vicinity; but such a situation for shipping purposes appears quite useless, and, I think, unless some insuperable obstacle exists, the township must be near the place which is most convenient for shipping and for the erection of wharves, and here the actual business of the Port must be carried on.

" In a straight line, I believe the chain of water holes is not more than one and a half to two miles from the present settlement, and before I left the Port a well of from thirty to thirty-five feet had been sunk in a ridge rather more than two-hundred yards back from the river, and from which very fair water had been obtained. From the width of the bed of the Mackay [Pioneer] the shortness of its course, the lowness of the opposite bank, and the close proximity of this position to the mouth of the river, I do not think that any flood can seriously affect the low bank from which the wharves will have to be built. There are, however, marks of small driftwood where it slightly falls just at the foot of the ridge, which is about two-hundred yards back from the bank of the river. This ridge is about thirteen feet above high water springs, and must be beyond all reach of floods, which, even on the low bank, cannot rise beyond a few inches and that only for a very short period of time during the top of high water. This elevation forms the commencement of a plain of about ten or fifteen miles in extent, composed of rich black soil and is intersected by the chain of water holes which I before mentioned.

Fig. 19.—The first Trinity Church (Church of England), It was built of stone but collapsed owing to defective foundations.

"There appears to be easy access to the interior from this port, thirty bales of wool arrived during my visit and I was informed by Mr. Alex. McLennan, a gentleman to whom a portion of it belonged, that it had taken him sixteen days to travel one hundred and thirty miles; but that now that he knew where to find water during his journey, he could in future safely calculate on doing it in eleven days, and that the only other impediment he encountered was at some creeks where the steep banks required cutting down. The gap over the range did not, he told me, present any serious difficulties—one slight siding only requiring to be cut. About £150 he considered would effect all that is required at present for making a good road to the settlement in the interior." Lieut. Heath gives sailing directions and calls attention to the "snags which are dangerous in the upper part of the river which ought to be removed at once, and which can be done with little difficulty as at low water they are quite easy of access."

In a communication to me on the subject in 1886, Commander Heath says: " There were four stores, two of them were large buildings of galvanized iron, and one [the principal one] of them was in charge of Mr. J. R. Palfryman. The principal store stood where the A. S. N. Co.'s store now stands [1886]; at that time the river bank extended a considerable distance in front of the store giving sufficient space to turn a team of bullocks between the river bank and the store. Mr. and Mrs. Conner lived near the bank of the river about two and a half miles away from the settlement. Mr. Conner had teams on the road."

The principal store referred to was that of Burns, Bassett & Co., and it stood on ground which has long since been washed away. In an advertisement in the *Port Denison Times*, in 1864, the situation is described as at the corners of Carlyle and River Streets. This store was erected in 1862; the owners were J. & W. Burns, of Parramatta, Dr. Bassett and the latters stepson, Sutherland In April, 1864, they transferred their business to McLeod, Carter & Co. On the 29th July, 1862, they

Fig. 20.—Thermometer Stand at The Hollow. C. C. Rawson on the left. The records obtained here were arranged by H. Ling Roth, and tabulated and published in the Journal of the Roy. Soc. of N. S. Wales, 1881. From a Photograph by E. S. Rawson.

had obtained the Government contract for conveying the mails by steam between Rockhampton and Port Denison for £100 per month, the mails from Sydney per brigantine "Mariposa," Capt. Hurley, arriving every five weeks.

Anderson, Burkitt, Tom Mathews, Dominic Negretti, Bolger, and others arrived in 1862. Anderson and Burkitt erected a store where J. P. Kemp afterwards had his bookselling and stationer's shop. Fleming, Voysey, Mr. and Mrs. Jeffers, arrived on 31st January, 1863.

After the "Presto" the arrivals at Mackay for several months were as follows:—s.s. "Murray" and the three-masted schooner "Policeman;" schooner "Marion Renny," Capt. M'Ewan; schooner "Henry Edward," Capt. Carter; schooner "Louisa Maria," Capt. Garcia. In the early days the passengers and cargo were landed off the boats on to the river bank, which was then situated in about the present mid-channel, and the visits of boats to the little bush town were uncertain, few and far between. All Government business had to be transacted at Bowen, and the difficulties of communication with that place rendered for a time compliance with the law a very expensive and often an impossible proceeding.

Following Lieut. Heath's survey, Mackay was on the 5th February, 1863, declared a "port of entry and clearance;" and shortly after this, about the 14th February, the s.s. "Murray" (previously mentioned), Capt. Till, arrived after an eight days' voyage from Rockhampton. The "Murray" was a wretched old craft, and had been twice compelled by the gale to put back to Keppel Bay, where, running short of provisions, the "Ocean Chief," Capt. Davis (she afterwards grounded in the bay in this gale and broke her back), gave her some assistance in the way of provisions. Owing it is said to the shortness of provisions amongst the steerage passengers there was an attempt at a riot on board, which was quickly nipped in the bud by the firmness of the Captain. Amongst other passengers on this journey up were Alex. Shiels, K. H. Wills (who went on to Bowen and afterwards owned Will's Hotel, Mackay), Charlie Keeley, Will Landels, W. Bagley, and John Tanner Baker—the first government official. The large number of passengers was due to the high terms

Fig, 21.—Alex. Shiels, Accountant. Proprietor of Shiels' Hotel.

in which some men from Fort Cooper, on arrival at Rockhampton, spoke of the agricultural lands of Mackay. These men had been shearing for A. Kemmis and E. B. Cornish, at Fort Cooper, where Bovey was storekeeper. Baker was Resident Officer of Customs and was afterwards appointed Police Magistrate at the request of Mr. Thornton; he occupied most of the government appointments. It is said that when the two first policemen came, in this year they did their night duty with rifles in their hands!

On January 9th, 1863, the Post Office was opened, and in July arrangements were in progress for connecting Mackay with other parts of the Colony by telegraph; it was proposed to run the line from St. Lawrence via Collaroy, Scott's, Bell's, Plane Creek, Greenmount to Bowen, with a branch from Greenmount to Mackay. In May the "Diamantina" s.s. ran on a snag in the Pioneer River, but got off; this led to the proposal to have the river cleared of snags, but it was not until May 15th, 1865, that tenders had to be in for "the removal, cutting up and burning of a number of snags, trees, etc., etc., being not less than fifty in number, now lying in or upon the banks of the Pioneer River."

The first sale of Mackay lands was held on the 1st of July, 1864, at Bowen, Port Denison. Of this land sale D. Conner writes me :—" The " Williams " steamer was expected to call at Mackay to take passengers up ; thinking the steamer might not put in an appearance in time I made up my mind to start overland. I tried to hunt up a mate, but had no success, so started alone. The wet season had set in, consequently all the rivers and creeks were flooded and full of alligators, the Blacks bad and numerous, the country boggy, and no track or road from St. Helens, forty miles from Mackay, so I had eighty miles of travel without a road. The most trying part of the trip was the want of companionship, especially at night when camping out without a fire, the mosquitoes in millions and not being able to sleep and praying for daylight. The first day I arrived at St. Helens, (Graham and J. and W. Macartney's Station,) and that night we had a most terrific cyclone; I never witnessed anything like it. It rained in torrents, very soon the roof blew off and at the end of three hours it left the station a perfect wreck. I arrived at J. W. McDonald's place, Adelaide Point, four miles from town, the day before the sale. Mr. McDonald drove me into Bowen the next morning where I attended the sale, being the only representative from Mackay, the "Williams" not having arrived. She put in an appearance three days after. I met several people in Bowen who later

Fig. 22.—The Hollow (Sleepy Hollow), Shamrock Vale, on the south bank of the Pioneer (C. C. Rawson). From a photograph taken in 1880. The old original house is the middle one shifted round from the site of the new house on the right, and turned into a kitchen, and afterwards into a store.

on came and settled in Mackay. Having had a full dose of overlanding I sold my horses at a very good figure and returned by the 'Williams.'" On October 12th, 1864, there was another Sale of Mackay Lands when good prices were realised. On August 4th of this year the first Mackay Court of Petty Sessions was held.

At the end of this year, 1864, Barker and Jas. and Rob. Martin took up Hamilton stocking it with cattle from Barker's Station, Walla, on the Burnett. The Martins had originally applied for The Hollow (called Abington by them) but had forfeited it, and in December of the following year, 1866, C. C. and E. S. Rawson purchased from Kemmis (agent for the mortgagee) 600 head of cattle, which were part of Mackay and Starr's original stock, and applied for a lease of the forfeited country, which was granted to them. "Hoppy" Moore (he was lame) was then in charge of The Hollow, and with him was Ned Kettle, afterwards of Peak Downs.

In the back country, sheep stations which had now been well established, were afterwards largely transformed into cattle stations owing to the prevalent "grass seed" (*Stipa sp.?*) which penetrated the wool and flesh of the sheep to their ultimate destruction.

Fig. 23.—J. Ewen Davidson, B.A., 1st Class Nat. Science, Oxon., 1862, a scion of the Davidsons of Tulloch Castle, Rossshire, a pupil and friend of the late Professor Rolleston, F.R.S. In 1865 he started sugar planting at Rockingham Bay, where he was flooded out. In connection with T. H. Fitzgerald he erected in 1868 the first sugar mill at Mackay (The "Alexandra" Plantation). He was the first Chairman of the Mackay Divisional Board. While at Rockingham Bay he collected various articles made by the natives which he presented to the British Museum, and discovered a new indigenous plum tree, with fine fruit and prickly stem, now known as *Davidsonia pruviens*. In 1888 he took up for recreation the study of Astronomy, aided by a fine 6-in. equatoreal telescope, originally sent out for the use of the Transit of Venus Expedition in 1882, with which he found a new comet, ' E,' on July 19th, 1889: the first to be discovered from the territory of Queensland.

The following stations, apart from those already referred to, were sending their produce to Mackay for shipment: St. Helens, founded by R. W. Graham and the brothers J. and W. Macartney (cousins of A. Macartney of Waverley); the Macartneys separated from Graham (who was in later times followed by Dyson Lacy), W. Macartney forming Bloomsbury Station (where J. C. Binney was superintendent until May, 1873, when he came to Mackay) and J. Macartney (known as Sir John Macartney, Bart.) formed Joliemont Station. Oxford Downs, J. W. Stuart; Blue Mountain, A. H. Lloyd; Wandoo and Bolingbroke, A. T. Ball; Homebush, Frank Bridgeman, nephew of E. B. Cornish; Grosvenor Downs, — Frazer; Burton Downs, R. M'Lennan; Suttor Creek, Robert Smith; Lake Elphinstone,* Alex. Ewen; Kelvin Grove, Mark (?) Christian; Plane Creek, Bell and Atherton; Skull Creek, Bailey, Newton and Liddiard; Tierawomba,—Scott; Newstead, —Wilmett; and Eaglefield, M. Hume Black, who afterwards owned the Cedars Sugar Plantation and represented Mackay in the Legislative Assembly—he was brother of Hy. Bowyer Black, co-founder and co-partner with E. J. Welch, R.N. of the *Mackay Standard.*

The first people to open an hotel, if such it could be called in Sydney Street, appear to have been Finger, Smith and O'Brien, who erected a small shanty on the spot where T. Hill's saddlery shop stood in 1884. They had no license and had arrived in the s.s. "Murray" in 1862, bringing a barmaid, named Jennie, with them. The second public house, or grog shanty, was that of Tom Mathews and Jeffries;—Jeffries was later on drowned in the Lagoons, having got stuck in the reeds whilst fishing. A.

---

* Selheim claimed to have discovered Lake Elphinstone and named it Lake Emilia, after his sister; but G. E. Dalrymple discovering it independently and without knowing anything about Selheim's claims, called it Lake Elphinstone. It is curious that Leichhardt's party should have passed so close to the lake without seeing it.

Henderson and Thos. Anderson sold grog at their stores.   Cridland's slab store (he does not appear to have sold grog) was situated between A. Henderson's and Finger, Smith and O'Brien's, which was at the back of Lobie's; Tom Mathews' was a little more to the west but somewhat in advance of Finger, Smith and O'Brien's and between that and the Golden Fleece.   Mrs. Cooke and Tommy Read had their grog shop behind Mathews'.*   Tommy Reid died from an overdose of laudanum whilst in Bowen in 1866.   The first license holders were Tommy Reid (brother of the well known Ellis Reid), Tom Mathews, A. Henderson and Jack O'Reilly—the latter got his license first but they all obtained licenses on the same day.†   The first real public house was that of Chas. Keeley, the Golden Fleece, afterwards Northey's Oriental Hotel.   Keeley was a pretty fair landlord and did much to try to prevent excessive drinking and lawlessness, and objected to a man "busting his cheque"

Fig. 24.—The original house at The Hollow (Sleepy Hollow), Shamrock Vale, built in 1866. (C. C. & E. S. Rawson.) This house afterwards became the Kitchen. E. S. Rawson in the foreground.

in his house.   On more than one occasion, when he saw too much drinking going on, he shut up the house; but once the "boys" were too much for him for they climbed up to the wall plates, and from the open space, between this and the open roof, for there was no ceiling, they pelted him and his wife in bed until he had to get up and re-open!

In these early days there was naturally some lawlessness, but it does not seem to have been very serious, nor of a character that could not have occurred in any settled town.   One of the first victims was a man of the name of Cope, known by the name of the "Wizard of the North."   Cope had taken more than was good for

---

* I have been told, but cannot find definite corroboration of the fact, that this shanty was called the Iron Pot. It was said to have been built of timber obtained from one Ti tree, had a low iron roof, and contained a slab counter in one piece 8 × 3 feet.   It was also said to have been built by Dominic Negretti.   Was it the Iron Hut?

† Jack O'Reilly was drowned at Dumbleton Crossing, about 1868.

him and was said to have been killed in a fight with a man named Kelly, whom he was accused of having robbed. Long Jack Johnson was one of the rowdy celebrities and, with others, he used to "boss" the town; he was a native Australian born, and a bullock driver at Fort Cooper, a brother-in-law of Robert Parr. He got lost in the bush and his body was found partially devoured by native dogs.

Fig. 25.—Captain William Robert Goodall, Police Magistrate. Previously to his appointment he had surveyed nearly the whole of the Kennedy District, naming the greater part of the hills and mounts; and before that he had served in the army and was in the China War of 1859, when he was wounded in the shoulder and had an eye knocked out. He was a very upright man and no respecter of persons, planter or labourer sharing alike. On one occasion, while presiding during a horsestealing case, a J.P. of doubtful character took his seat on the bench, whereupon Captain Goodall turned to him with the remark: " Good morning, Mr. B . . . , are you for the plaintiff or for the defendant ?" He was, however, too just and impartial to please everybody, and when a new Ministry got into power he was removed.

There is a very pretty story of the locking up of the first Police Magistrate who came to the town. It is said that having heard much about the Mackay "boys" he gave it out that he would soon settle them. Unfortunately for him some Mackay "boys" were on board. They heard him but "lay low," and when he was being shewn the town, and came to the Lock-up, he was run in and not allowed out until he had apologised.*

There was a Sale of Town Lots in February, 1865, at the Police Office. In January of this year the provisions of the Towns Police Act were extended to Mackay. That the district was beginning to thrive may be seen from the fact that the following vessels were trading to Mackay, viz.:—The " Eva," schooner, Capt. Macbeath; the " Percy," schooner, Capt. McEwen; the " Mary Williams," Capt. S. McBurney; " Briton's Queen," Capt. M. R. Brown; the " Amy," Capt. Wm. Major; the " Three Friends," Capt. Howe. On the 23rd June Mr. T. B. Yates road engineer, was found on the banks of the Pioneer River insensible, and expired in a few moments. He had only come down from Bowen the day before, and had left the ship apparently in good health.

In the early part of this year, 1865, the country had been startled by an outrage which had its sequel at Mackay. On Friday, 4th March, three men: Dawson, Manns (? M. Mahon) and McPherson attempted to murder R. H. Willis at the Haughton River. McPherson was caught and was being brought south for trial by the " Diamantina " steamer, in charge of a constable named Maher. On the night of the 24th June,

* Later on there was the " River Mob," who were the cattle men or station owners on and near the River, who, when they came down to Port for their mail once a month, made things lively in the town during their stay. They always ended their visits with a " bottle chorus," much to the annoyance of the Police Magistrate, as this usually took place about 4 a.m. The bottle chorus was a sailor's chanty—" Whisky for my Johnnie," " Rio Grande," etc., etc., accompanied by each man drawing an empty bottle down the side of a weatherboard house in imitation of hauling in ropes.

while the vessel was lying at Mackay, the constable, nothwithstanding the remonstances of the officers of the ship, humanely removed the prisoners' handcuffs and then fell asleep. McPherson naturally made his escape! His chains were afterwards found pinned to a tree a short distance from the town. He secured a pair of pistols from a station, and stole a horse from a blackboy in the service of Kemmis and Bovey. On the 4th November the "Wild Scotchman," as he was now called, crossed the Condamine, about six miles above the town of that name, and on January 2nd, 1866, he was said to have been seen at Sandgate; in the month of February, 1866, he

Fig. 26.—Charles Collinson Rawson.   Fig. 27.— Edmund Stansfeld Rawson.

Sons of Chas. Stansfeld Rawson of Wastdale Hall, Cumberland, formerly of the Hon. East India Company's Service, in which service his uncle Christopher Rawson, of Halifax, greatly distinguished himself*. Admiral Sir Harry Rawson, G.C.B., the present Governor of New South Wales, is a great nephew of Christopher Rawson. C C. and E. S. Rawson were joined by their cousin Harry Redesdale James,† son of Thos. James, of Otterburn Tower, Northumberland, and later on by their brother Lancelot Bernard Rawson, afterwards Crown Lands Ranger at Rockhampton, where he died in 1899.

stuck up the Peak Downs Mail. He was caught and was sentenced at Maryborough on the 13th September, 1866, to 25 years for robbery under arms, but was released on 22nd December, 1874. In the meanwhile, on 25th July, 1865, at Bowen, before Messrs. Pinnock, Cuthbert, Dillon, Macdonald Scott and Goodall, the constable (Maher) was sentenced to six months hard labour for allowing McPherson to escape!

It was on the first of June, 1865, that John Spiller put in the first sugar cane at Mackay. This was on the north side of the river. He had been to Java to learn sugar growing and manufacture, which knowledge he gained on the fine estate of Herr Moddeman, Pasoeroean, not far from Sourabaya. From Java Spiller brought 30,000 "plants" to Melbourne, where on arrival, owing to the long voyage of fifty-nine days, many of the plants were beginning to wither and decay. He therefore

* See *The Yorkshire Coiners, with Notes on Old and Prehistoric Halifax* by H. Ling Roth, Halifax, 1906

† Lost in the Petrel in Dec. 1873, together with Jack Firebrace, George Ramsay and Geo. Long (brother of E. M. Long).

left nearly the whole lot with the Hon. Capt. Louis Hope of Cleveland Bay, south of Brisbane, who planted them and sent Spiller half of the produce. In the meanwhile Spiller arrived at Mackay, and on tramping about on the north side of the river was struck by the luxuriant growth of the native grasses. To use his own words : " I always remember so well the grass being so high there by my Javanese boy and myself being very much startled by a bullock rushing past us and we could not see, but afterwards picked up its tracks. The first grass I burnt was on the Pioneer and it was 12-feet and over in height; it was what is known in Java as sugar grass, it contained saccharine and was quite sweet at the joints. It was here that I compared the young growth of grass to a lovely meadow ten days after the burning. I could see the fire burning in the Ranges for four days afterwards." He lived in a grass humpy and had his cane plants in a garden about forty yards square fenced round the hut. But Spiller while waiting for his plants to multiply turned his attention to maize and cotton and sent thirteen bales of cotton to Brisbane, reaping like few others in Mackay and elsewhere, the Government bonus of 4d. per lb. He also grew and sold, in one season, 6,000 bushels of maize which he sold to Hatfield, of Broadsound, at 6/- per bushel free on board, Mackay. In 1866, by arrangement, Spiller allowed T. H. Fitzgerald to have part of the crop due to him from Capt. Hope; Fitzgerald also obtained some plants from Capt. Whish at Redland Bay, and with these he planted a piece of ground near the R.C. Schools. In the following

Fig. 28.—John Spiller, a Devonshire man, planted the first sugar cane at Port Mackay —1st June, 1865. He formed the Pioneer Estate, and later on bought from the A. J. S. Bank the River Estate and worked that.

year the cane had multiplied so that Fitzgerald could begin operations on a larger scale. D. Conner who had arrived in Mackay in April, 1863, and had started carrying on the roads, was the first to put in the plough for cane, having taken a contract from Fitzgerald to plough and harrow 20 acres of land close to the Alexandra Mill. At the end of June, 1867, Spiller, with the help of a Mr. Booth from Java, put up a wooden horse mill with which he crushed some cane and boiled down the juice to sugar in an ordinary boiler, thus producing the first sugar in the district. But the mill was continually breaking down and he only managed to produce a few lbs. In the meanwhile John Ewen Davidson went into partnership with Fitzgerald and put up the first iron mill at the Alexandra in 1868; he crushed the first cane on 28th September, finishing on November 18th, producing 110 tons of sugar, thus proving the manufacture of sugar to be a commercial success.

* It has often been said that a horse power was put up at the Alexandra in order to irrigate sugar cane. This horse power was, I believe, afterwards used to pump water at the Alexandra, but never used for irrigation. The dam at the Palms Creek, which has often been mixed up with this irrigation scheme, was not put up till 1873, and was intended by Fitzgerald to supply a distillery on the river bank receiving molasses from the north side by means of pipes.

We must now go back to the year 1865 and see what was going on then. Sport was not forgotten. The first Race Meeting was held on the 29th, 30th June, 1865, with the following results :—First day, Hack Race (15 guineas), Minto, under protest ; Town Plate (40 guineas), Trimmer's Sydney ; Publican's Purse (30 guineas), Boyd's Manfred. Second day :—Ladies' Cup, with 10 guineas added, Trimmer's Sydney ; Hurdle Race, of 30 guineas, Ball's Bachelor ; Consolation Stakes (19 guineas) Ball's Granby. Ball rode in the hurdle race and broke his collar bone on the last hurdle ; Bob Bridgman was seriously injured. Francis Louis Meynell won the race.

Frank Smith (Solicitor).   H. Brandon (Manager A. J. S. Bank).   Geo. Smith (Shipping Agent).
Mrs. Brandon.   Percy Crees (Nephew J. Spiller).   Mrs. G. Smith.
Mrs. F. Smith.   John Spiller.   Mrs. Spiller.

Fig. 29.—The original " Pioneer " Plantation House, belonging to John Spiller, pulled down in 1878.

In the following month, July, Brodziak and Rodgers started a store, which afterwards passed into the hands of H. and E. Bromberg, nephews of Brodziak. Another large store was opened on the 25th November by McBryde Bros., the owners, who were represented by Jas. McBryde.

In August the road party clearing a road over the range, under the superintendence of Holmes, removed to Waverley and it was afterwards stated that on arrival there a nugget was found in the nose bag of one of the horses. In November a man named Ward, who had been a miner in Victoria, and who was now a sheep overseer at New Fort Cooper Station, W. S. Walker, found a nugget of gold whilst crossing a gully. His refusal to acquaint the shearers and station hands as to the whereabouts of the find led to disturbances.

In July the Custom House was erected, and we find that land was being taken up largely for sugar.   On October 13th the Governor of Queensland, Sir Geo. Bowen, who had been up the Coast before, arrived in the "Platypus," Capt. Champion, in company with the Hon. John Douglas, and was presented with an address.   A supper was given in his honour in the store room of the Golden Fleece Hotel at 9 p.m.   Thirty-eight guests sat down.   T. H. Fitzgerald and R. A. Goldring were "chair" and "vice" and Douglas proposed a separate member to represent Mackay.   The Governor left the same night.

Willie Bell,
on the Fence.   Fig. 30.—Plane Creek Station Homestead (Henry Bell).   Mount Chelona in the
background.

In this year, 1865, Elphinstone township was started.   It was not a success.

While the town of Mackay was thus growing in importance, we may take a glance again at the progress the settlement of the immediate surrounding country had been making, and a very good idea of this can be gathered from the particulars of the fortnightly Mail Service from Rockhampton to Port Denison which were as follows :—*

				miles.	
To Yaamba	...	...	...	28	
„ Princhester ...	...	...	—		Van Wessen.

* Many of the names were wrongly spelled in *Pugh's Almanac* for 1863 ; they are corrected here.

			miles.	
To Marlborough	...	...	42	Henning and Winter, outside Post Office to the north.
„ Tooloomba ...	...	...	28	Douglas' Accommodation House.
„ Waverley ...,	...	...	31	J. A. Macartney.
„ Collaroy	...	...	40	Fitz and Conner.
„ Meiklejohns	...	...	12	Meiklejohn.
„ Newstead ...	...	...	30	Wilmot and Woolley.
„ Fort Cooper	...	...	40	Kemmis and Cornish.
„ Exmoor, Bowen River	...	75	Henning.
„ Strathmore	do.	...	36	P. Selheim and Toussaint.
„ Eaton Vale ...	...	...	22	Collins and McDonald.
„ Bowen	...	...	40	
	Total	...	424	Miles.

Fig. 31.—The "Alexandra" Plantation House, from the Garden,
(J. Ewen Davidson.)

The route was not by any means a straight one and gives a fair idea of the then occupation of the country. Marlborough had originally been taken up by Conner, and Newstead by Bridges, and Strathmore by Toussaint. Turner Bros. and Anslow were nearer the coast north of Waverley. The road stock took was from Waverley across Conner's Range to Collaroy, 40 miles, crossing Boothill, Funnell, Denison and Nebo Creeks to Fort Cooper, 70 miles. In his Almanac for 1866 Pugh gives a more extended list of the post stations and adds interesting notes of the occupation of the country on either side of the route.

" Mails from Rockhampton to Port Denison are conveyed by steamer as opportunity offers, but the overland route, which is fortnightly, is maintained in order to supply the large number of stations on the line with the advantages of mail communication.

Victoria Street.   Sydney Street.

Fig. 32.—A. Shiels' Hotel, burnt down in 1872.   It was situated at the corners of Victoria Street and Sydney Street, where Ricketts Hotel was afterwards erected, and where the premises of the Union Bank of Australia now stand.

Cooks "Standard"   Wills   Victoria   Geo. Ricketts
Hotel.   McKenney, Saddler.   Hotel.   Street.   Hotel.

Fig. 33.—Sydney Street in 1876, looking towards the river.   Wills' and Ricketts Hotels are at the corners of Victoria Street   The site of Ricketts Hotel became that of the Union Bank of Australia afterwards.

Fig. 34.—View of Sydney Street, in 1876, looking south. *i.e.* from river bank, with Trinity Church at the extreme top.   The two storied brick building is Sharp's Red House, the house next to it was occupied by the A. J. S. Bank when they removed in from the bush (and before they bought the premises in Victoria Street, next to Ricketts Hotel).

Stations, &c.		Miles.	Owners, Locality, &c.
Rockhampton to Yaamba	...	23	North side of Fitzroy.
Thence to Canoona	... ...	8	Former diggings.
,, Princhester...	...	22	Van Wessen.
,, Marlborough	...	10	Henning and Winter.
,, Langdale, Tooloombah		28	J. Douglas.
,, Waverley ...	...	28	J. A. Macartney.
,, Lotus Creek	...	35	Fitzsimmons and Sheridan.
,, Cardowan ...	...	18	Wilmots.
,, Cardossan ...	...	—	
,, Funnell Creek	...	38	Do.
,, Nebo Creek	...	18	Reynolds' Inn.*
,, Fort Cooper	...	7	Kemmis and Cornish.
,, Blenheim ...	...	58	E. Lack's.
,, Exmoor ...	...	13	Henning's.
, Crossing, Bowen	...	20	Public House.
, Sonoma ...	...	12	Paterson and Landsborough.
,, Bogie Hotel	...	28	
,, Eurie Creek	...	17	Clark's Public House.
,, Don River ...	...	13	
, Bowen ...	...	10	Port Denison.
	Total ...	406	

" At Tooloombah, within a short distance of the station, there is a public house ; and at Waverley there is one kept by Messrs. Wallace and M'Gusty, and situated half a mile from this side of Waverley Station, and at the point where the Port Denison Road branches off. St. Lawrence is the shipping port of Broad Sound, and is four and a half miles from Waverley, off the road, so that the postman has to go nine miles out of his way in going there. There is an inn at St. Lawrence, kept by a Mr. Boyce. Clairview is 17 miles from Waverley, and four from the sea coast ; Yatton, late Mr. Cobham's, is 17 miles south of Lotus Creek, and 40 miles north of Apis Creek; May Downs, Mr. Arthur M'Kenzie's, is 12 miles S.W. of Yatton ; Arthur Downs, Mr. M'Henry's, is 40 miles W. by S. of Yatton, 45 W.S.W. of Lotus Creek, and 20 from Cotherstone ; the last mentioned station is 35 miles from Gordon Downs, and 35 from Retro Creek. From Lotus Creek to Conner's River is a distance of 13 miles ; thence to Cardowan, five miles ; thence to junction of main road six miles ; thence (towards Collaroy) to the crossing-place, three miles ; thence to Boundary Creek, four miles ; thence—leaving the main road, going through a gap, and crossing the river again—to Collaroy, a distance of three miles.

" At the old station of Fort Cooper, the roads to Mackay, Port Denison, the Thompson, the heads of the Isaacs, Rockhampton and Peak Downs meet. From Fort Cooper to the range which divides the waters of the Isaacs from those of the Bowen, is a distance of 20 miles ; across the range, 10 miles ; thence to the crossing-place of the Bowen, 20 miles, Mr. Hilfling's station (Havilah) is about seven miles from the crossing-place.† Mr. Lack's station is about a mile and a half off the road,

* Reynolds, of Fort Cooper Hotel, died in June, 1867.

† Havilah was taken up by Hilfling and Peterson in 1861; they afterwards came to Mackay and Henderson bought the station.

9

Fig. 35 —" Branscombe " Plantation House in 1879   Built by the brothers E. M. Long (afterwards of " Habana " Plantation) and Geo. Long (drowned in the " Petrel " in 1873) and G. N. Marten of St. Albans, England.   Purchased by G. H. M. King.

F. T. Amhurst's Room.   Bob Walker's Room.   Ling Roth's Room.

Fig. 36.—" Foulden " Plantation House, from a photograph taken in 1881.   Built (about 1875) by Francis Tyssen Amhurst, M.L.A. (brother of Lord Amherst of Hackney).

Master F. J. M. King.

Fig. 37.—Fryerne. (G. H. M. King.)   Built in 1883, destroyed by fire in 1888.
From a photograph by G. H. M. King.

up Blenheim Creek. The distance from this point to Port Mackay (Pioneer River) is 65 miles as the crow flies.

Fig. 38.—W. Purves, the first Town Clerk.

Fig. 40,—C. W. Toussaint took up Strathmore. He came to the Colony in 1856 or 1859, afterwards taking Selheim into partnership, later on becoming manager at Oxford Downs, and afterwards for the Finch Hattons at Mount Spencer (The Retreat) Hazelwood and Blue Mount. Lastly he was manager for the Rawsons at The Hollow, He came from Hanau or Wilhelmsbad in Hesse Cassel, and was a connection of Prince Schweichhardt. He belonged to an old Hugenot family which was driven out of France, where it originally held considerable property near Amiens and Diedenhofen (Dijon). He was educated at the Hohenheim Agricultural College, and was once manager of the Rothschild estate, Gut Lenthof. His grandfather lent money to Beniofsky (who was drowned in the retreat across the Elster) and going later to St. Petersburg was sent to the mines in Siberia, where after seven years detention a travelling friend recognised him and obtained his release. C. W. T.'s younger brother died of cholera and his elder brother, who went to Ohio just before the war, has never since been heard of. Amongst his friends he was popularly known as " The Relic," an abreviation of "That Old Foreign Relic." He was an excellent judge of farm stock. He died in February, 1903.

Fig. 39.—Frank Kinchant. The first man to get married at Mackay. He married J. & R. Martin's sister, 18 Mar., 1867. Mount Kinchant was named after him.

"A. Macdougall has a station on Bowen Plains, near the crossing place over the Bowen.—From Burnett's station (formerly Stuart's), on Peak Downs, to Cotherstone,

J. Thorne's, is 25 miles; thence to Logan Downs, M'Laren and M'Donald's, 35 miles; thence to Grosvenor Downs, Frazer Brothers, 28 miles; thence to Burton Downs, Raymond, Fitz and Fetherstonhaugh's, on the Isaacs, 35 miles.—Eaglefield, on the Suttor, Dr. Wilkin's, is 27 miles from Burton Downs; thence to Lockerwood, same owner, 25 miles; thence to Newlands, same owner (adjoining Kirk and Sutherland's) 12 miles.

"From Burton Downs to Lake Elphinstone, Mr. Alex. M'Ewan's, the distance is 10 miles; thence to Fort Cooper, 33 miles. Messrs Kirk and Sutherland have a station 40 miles west of Fort Cooper, and 18 west of Lake Elphinstone.—From Henning's (Exmoor) to the junction of Broken River is six miles, and thence to crossing place over the Bowen, 14 miles. Mr. Palmer has a station on Pelican Creek. Strathmore (Mr. Sellheim's) is 12 miles from the range between the Bogie and Bowen Waters, and 13 miles from the public-house at the crossing-place of the

Fig. 41.—The Hon. D. H. Dalrymple ("Dal"), M.L.A., first Mayor of Port Mackay.

Fig. 42.—Joseph Holmes started Pleystowe, where he grew Cotton in 1867—1868.

Bogie. Eton Vale, the station of Messrs. Collins and Macdonald, is near to the public-house, and about 20 miles from Strathmore.

"Stockyard Creek, a camping-place is 10 miles from the crossing at the Bogie; thence to Ewri Creek, a public-house, seven miles; and thence to the Don, 13 miles.

"At the crossing-place over the Don, on the ordinary road, there are two inns, distant from which Mr. Bode* has a station two miles,—the Police Baracks four miles; from the latter to Bowen the distance is six miles.

"On Rosella Creek, above Hilfling's, Dr. Wilkin has a station, and near to him Mr. Arch. Ferguson has also a station.†

"The gradual opening up of shipping ports to the northward is giving a better opportunity to settlers for choice as to which shall be the place of shipment for their

---

* Strathdon, which he took up following Dalrymple's second trip. He took up Bromby Park with Dangar in 1866 or 1867.

† Byerwen, which was taken up by Joe Walker who stocked it with sheep.

produce. The subjoined stations are among those which ship their wool either from Broad Sound or Pioneer River:—Yatton, late Cobham's; A. M'Kenzie, of the Isaacs River; Fitzsimmons and Sheridan, Lotus Creek; Skinner & Murmin, of Amity Creek; Clairview, Broad Sound; Turner Brothers, Broad Sound; M'Laren, of Collaroy; Wilmot, of Funnell Creek; Hazlewood. A. T. Ball; Robert Lawson, of Oxford Downs; Munro, on the North Creek, a tributary of the Isaacs. The road drays usually take is from Waverley to Lotus Creek, and thence across the range to Wilmot's, at Funnell Creek, and thence by Denison and Nebo Creeks to Fort Cooper." The Mackay and Nebo service (fortnightly) was:—

		Miles.
Mackay to Greenmount, John Walker (How, Walker & Co.)...		13
Thence to W. Bagley's Public House		12
,, Jas. Ready's Do.		12
,, Retreat (Station)		12
,, Heineman's Public House		$1\frac{1}{2}$
,, Nebo (post town at Fort Cooper)...		18
	Total Miles ...	$68\frac{1}{2}$

Fig. 43.—Mrs. Cooke's Royal Hotel, Sydney Street.

Although in the matter of crime and financial troubles Mackay had some hard knocks during the year 1866, still the year began prosperously and saw the commencement of that development of the manufacture of Sugar which was ultimately to become the staple industry of the district. On April 5th, W. O. Hodgkinson, explorer and afterwards Gold Fields Warden, began the issue of the *Mackay Mercury*. It was the first newspaper and was printed at the Golden Fleece. Hodgkinson, Munro and Drury had started the *News* in Rockhampton, in opposition to the *Bulletin* which had been first issued on June 9th, 1861, but they 'bust' over it. The Mackay public purchased the *News* plant for Hodgkinson, a pound subscription entitling the subscriber to a copy of the new weekly paper, the *Mercury*, free for ten months.

The Golden Fleece was by now a well established institution where all the most important meetings took place. On April 26th, a meeting was held there, A. Kemmis in the chair, when it was decided that the Government should proclaim Mackay a warehousing port (proposed by A. Shiels and seconded by R. A. Goldring). It was also decided to ask the A. S. N. Co. to reduce the freight on wool to £1 per bale. The memorials were drawn up by J. Allen. As a result of the petition to the Government, Mackay was declared a warehousing port on the 5th of November. By June, the progress of the telegraph installation had progressed so far that Brown and Sherry, the Contractors, started stretching the telegraph wires, and the line was practically open on 11th August, but the Office was not opened until 6th September. On June 23rd, W. Slocum was killed at Fort Cooper by the bough of a falling tree; on June 28th, Land Sales were held, and on July 11th Thos. A. Anderson, one of the earliest Mackay residents was drowned in the loss of the s.s. "Cawarra" off Newcastle (N.S. Wales). Cotton was planted this year, the first to grow it being Jos. Holmes at Pleystowe, but unfortunately the rains came down when the cotton was in pod and destroyed it. In parenthesis it may be remarked that Holmes built the wharf

Fig. 44.—Jim Martin of Hamilton Station, brother of Bob Martin, son of Dr. Martin of Leadhills, Lanarkshire. He could carry a 200-lb sack of flour, under each arm, up a flight of steps. He could also drink water placed 6-inches below his feet without bending his knees. His height was 6-ft. 4-in.

at the foot of Brisbane Street and also the old Sawn Bridge on the Nebo Road, under the Superintendance of Fitzgerald; he and Alex. Jardine cut the new road over the range. It was in this year, that the Leichhardt Hotel at Lake Elphinstone was erected by Clerke, who, on returning from Burton Downs, was afterwards found dead, his horse coming home alone. In after years this hotel was pulled down and the timbers used in its re-erection at one of the corners of River Street, Mrs. Ronald, formerly Mrs. Reynolds of Nebo, being the proprietor.

Having now come to the end of the year when the establishment of the local press makes it possible to trace the progress of the district from printed records, there is no need to proceed further, and I will close the account of the establishment of the town and district with a description of an event which caused considerable commotion at the time, viz. :—

THE "STICKING UP" OF THE MACKAY BRANCH OF THE

AUSTRALIAN JOINT STOCK BANK.

In September, the whole district was put into a state of excitement by the sticking up of the Australian Joint Stock Bank*, and the following account of what took place is extracted from the *Mackay Mercury* of the 19th September, 1866:

* This Branch was opened on the 30th Jannary, 1866.

One of the first uses to which the local telegraph has been put was to inform the General Manager of the Australian Joint Stock Bank, that the Mackay Branch of that Institution had been robbed to the tune of some hundreds of pounds. The details of the theft are as follows:

About a quarter to twelve on Wednesday, the 12th instant, as Mr. Geddes, the Manager, was sitting in his room, Mr. Green, the Accountant, being at a small table behind the counter, the latter saw two men, an American mulatto and a native apparently, coming up the pathway which leads through a thick low scrub to the Bank door, Mr. Green said, " Who is this coming?" Mr. Geddes replied, " I do not know." The men then walked in, turned to the counter, and the dark one pulling out a £1 note asked for change. Mr. Green said, " How will you have it, half a sovereign and the rest in silver?" " I want all silver" said the man. While Mr. Green was stooping down to count it out the other man said, " Are you Mr. Green?" " Yes," said the latter. " Then where is Mr. Geddes?" " There he is " said Green, pointing to the Manager. Having thus identified their men, the native moved towards the Manager's room and stopping for a moment behind the partition, pulled out a revolver and presenting it at Geddes said, " If you stir, you're a dead man." The dark fellow then covered Green, saying, " Don't you stir." The Manager and Accountant were then ordered into a small room behind the counter, the native keeping guard over them while the half-caste closed the bank door and searched for plunder, taking all the gold, notes and silver he could find, with the exception of six unissuable notes. The money he stowed away in a bag, the native in the meanwhile relieving the tedium of the prisoners by offering them an apple each. Having, however, but one, he had to tax the good nature of his mate for a second, the latter temporarily suspending his cash transactions while he pulled the fruit from his pouch. When the prisoners had been consoled with an apple, the native pulled out a second pistol and held one in each hand at his prisoners. A little friendly conversation then ensued. Mr. Green somewhat naively remarking, " We little expected a visit from you this morning, you took us quite unawares." " I suppose not," replied the native. Green then said, " It is a d——d shame to rob us, it is only a small Bank, and we are just commencing business." To this the unanswerable response was, " We want the money and must have it." By this time the half-caste had nearly finished pillaging the drawers, and Mr. Green asked him not to touch the cheques or papers as they would be of no use to him and only disarrange the accounts. Mr. Geddes backed up this observation by stating that they bore the Bank stamp, and that as they (the bushrangers) had all the money they ought to be satisfied. The half-caste was apparently satisfied for he left the cheques and papers untouched, and was turning away when his mate asked, " Have you looked into the safe?" Mr. Geddes, pointing to the *teller's* safe, said, " Here it is," and Mr. Green opening it also invited them to look in. They did so, and seeing nothing but a couple of bills, shut it, observing, " We have got everything." " Then you had better be off," said Geddes, and off they went after the usual caution that if their victims gave the alarm for half an hour they would shoot them. Mounting their horses, which during the whole time had been tied to the post of the fence, they leisurely passed two or three cottages, several teams just then coming into Mackay, and cleared off with £746 8s. as the product of their daring coolness.

Such are the facts of the robbery as communicated to us, and having narrated these facts we superadd what follows from our personal knowledge of the circumstances :—

Clearly to comprehend the ease with which the theft was committed at noon, within twenty yards of the highroad, our readers must bear in mind that the Bank is situated in a secluded spot, and bounded by sugar canes, bushes and scrub, almost concealing it from view. There are, it is true, houses on three sides within earshot, and the fence to which the bushrangers' horses were tied lies some thirty yards from the Bank door. A few yards lower down the road again is a cottage occupied by Mr. Gogay, a butcher's shop, fifty or a hundred yards below that, and sundry other residences dotting either side of the road for half a mile. On leaving the Bank the men had to walk to their horses, in view of Mr. Gogay, to avoid exciting suspicion by undue haste to get on their horses, and for three miles at least to travel within view of the town, the road running over a bare plain unincumbered by timber. The Bank officials were left unbound, one at least with a revolver. Why in the name of common sense did one or both not give the alarm by calling out, firing a shot on the chance of frightening the bushrangers' horses or what not? So far from such being the case, the very fact of the Bank being stuck up was treated as a jest for some ten minutes, the Manager running, revolver in hand, down the town with trigger cocked and hair erect as he gasped forth the fact to the Acting Police Magistrate. As usual in such cases, not a horse was to be got, the police were running about one way, volunteers another, the sergeant had no cartridges, the volunteers no stomach to exert themselves for the welfare of a Bank, the Manager of which declined to assume the responsibility of paying reasonable expenses or offering a reward. At length, the Sergeant of Police, Messrs. Binney, Green, Fraser and Hodgkinson mounted in pursuit, and reached Bagley's Hotel, twenty miles from Mackay, just in time to learn that the bushrangers, after taking a bottle of beer, had inquired the road to Rockhampton, and turned off on to a side track that runs from Bagleys. Down this side track then rushed the sergeant and volunteers, but after going five miles, Messrs. Hodgkinson and Fraser retraced their steps to Fort Cooper, and learnt that they were on the right scent, the bushrangers having been met by the mailman, Mr. Mitchell, of Mitchell & Phiftu, and others. To cut a long story short, the horses of the volunteers knocked up, they did not feel justified in incurring further expenses to be disavowed by the Bank on their return, so they gave up the pursuit which was spiritedly continued by the sergeant, assisted by special constables; but the bushrangers turned off the Fort Cooper Road, near Ready's, and were last seen making towards Bluemount (A. H. Lloyd's) for Rockhampton, via Waverley.

The two men implicated can be easily identified. Only a short time since they stuck up the Lirchhardt Hotel, at Lake Ulphinstone; at that time there were three in the gang, and a report is current, which, however, we do not credit, that they have put their third mate out of the way. . . . . On the evening previous to the robbery, Mr. J. T. Baker had paid £450 to the Bank on Government account, and that the affair was well planned and long meditated is evident from the fact that the two men were seen lurking near the Bank on Monday, and when asked by Mr. Keeley what they wanted, said "change." No doubt they would have committed the theft then but for Mr. Keeley's appearance, and had they done so they would have obtained less plunder by £450.

It appears that on Sunday Evening, Messrs. Geddes and Green were returning to the Bank, accompanied as far as the gate by two other residents, when a low whistle, re-echoed by a second from another quarter, attracted their attention, and naturally enough excited the suspicions of all present. Stepping cautiously up the

PART OF MAP
OF
QUEENSLAND
FROM THE
SURVEYOR GENERAL'S
MAP, SHEET 2.

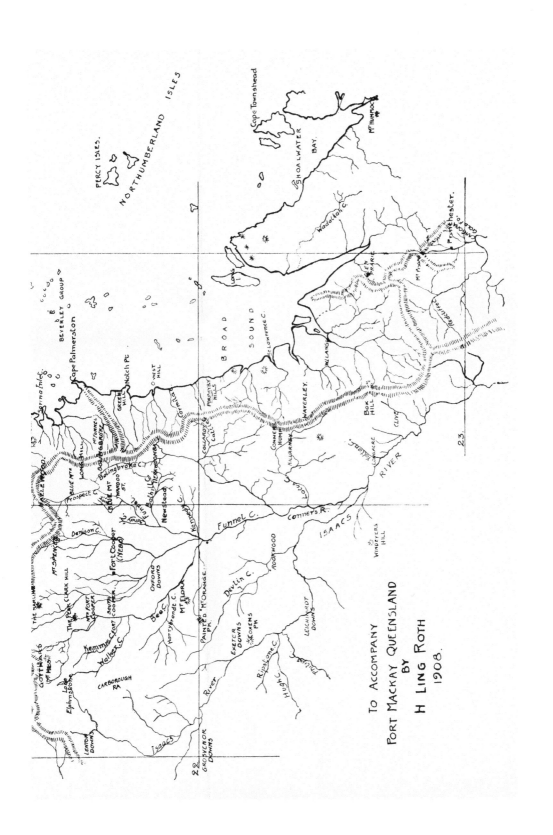

TO ACCOMPANY
PORT MACKAY QUEENSLAND
BY
H LING ROTH
1908.

side path, a man was apparently seen trying to force the lock of the side door of the Bank. Mr. Geddes drew his revolver immediately, but being recommended not to fire too hastily, the party rushed up, seized the intruder and found it to be a "dummy" dressed up with much ingenuity.

The remainder of the story is taken from the *Armidale Express* of the 27th October in the same year.

Our Inverell correspondent writing on the 23rd, announces the capture of two of the men who stuck up the Mackay Branch of the Australian Joint Stock Bank on the 12th September last, getting clear off with £746. There names are, Henry Ford, alias Billy Billy, and William Chambers, [? Chandler] alias Yellow Billy.

I am not able (says the writer) to exhibit every link in the chain of circumstances that led to the arrest of those scoundrels for they are both secured, nor are all the facts relating to the capture of such yet known to a single individual, but what follows may be depended on as reliable. It seems that Sergeant Doherty, of Warialda, was two or three days ago on a journey to the Barwan, and, whilst stopping for refreshment at a public-house on the way, he noticed an unusual plethora of the circulating medium in the shape of gold and bran new bank notes, and, being somewhat curious in the matter, he made known his observations to the landlord, remarking that they of Warialda scarcely ever saw money in any other shape than that of cheques and orders. The latter then let the inquisitive sergeant into the secret by informing him that he had the good luck to entertain for a short time lately, two young fellows who were not only possessed of becoming spirit, but also the wherewithal to maintain it, which they did right merrily whilst under his roof. On getting a description of the men, he at once recollected he had met them, and immediately connected them in his own mind with the robbery in Queensland, of which he had read an account but a few hours before. He then, without loss of time, wrote to the police at Moree, describing the men and giving his suspicions. The letter led, I believe, to the arrest of one of them, for in the meantime they had parted company. This one was secured in a rather novel manner. The police came upon him while asleep, handcuffed him, and withdrew from his belt a formidable revolver without ever disturbing his innocent slumbers. On finding that one was secured, Doherty set himself about tracking the other, which he did to Inverell, in company with Constable M'Dowell. Upon arriving here on Saturday, he let Senior Constable Farnsworth into the secret of his visit. They then went to the several public-houses, ostensibly to noblerise, but really all eyes for their game, which they failed to discover just then. Senior Constable Farnsworth, to whom Chandler is well-known, next suggested a likely place some miles from town, and where it seems the predatory mulatto had an affair of the heart, but to make sure he was not in the township they crossed the river about twilight to have a glance into Lunney's public-house, which is in an isolated position from the township. As soon as Farnsworth entered the bar he saw his man, who, upon recognising him, cordially held out his hand with a "How are you, Mr. F.?" "Oh, how do you do, Chandler?" replied Farnsworth. He retained Farnsworth's hand until he had pulled him up to the counter and called for nobblers. Just then Doherty, unobserved, slipped in and whispered in Farnsworth's ear, "Is this he?" and upon getting an answer in the affirmative he laid his hand on Chandler, saying, "You are my prisoner." The latter at once thrust his hand into his pocket and drew a revolver, which Senior Constable Farnsworth immediately seized by the muzzle with his left hand, and with the other drew his own and struck his prisoner three or four fearful blows on the head piece with it, which had the effect of bringing him to the floor with Doherty under him. In the meantime Constable Cunningham had joined them, and it was as much as all four could do to keep him down and prevent him using the weapon. As Doherty lay under the monster, his efforts were restricted to holding on by the wool of his head, which is rather profuse. Cunningham and M'Dowell were straining every nerve to keep him down and wrench from his hand the pistol which he held with a death gripe, and the muzzle of which he continually kept striving at one or other of his assailants, but Farnsworth at the imminent risk of his life manfully retained his hold on it, and continued to guide it in a harmless direction. Whilst things were in this position, the difficulty was how to get the handcuffs on, for every one had as much as he could do. At last Senior Constable Farnsworth dropped his own revolver and managed to get them attached to one arm and then with some difficulty on the other. This operation was performed with one hand as the other was doing important service in holding the muzzle of Chandler's revolver. The worst was now over; they soon wrenched the weapon from his grasp, and escorted him to the lock-up. On searching his person they got £12 10s. od. in gold and 6/3 in silver, and in his swag £305 in notes, making a sum total of £317 16s. 3d. Chandler was taken to Wariada yesterday (Monday) morning, escorted by Senior Constable Farnsworth, Sergeant Doherty, and Constable M'Dowell. He is a mulatto, and a strong powerful fellow.

It was current opinion at the time that these two men had a mate named Alex. Stuart, with whom they were seen two or three days before the bank robbery at Budgen's Hotel, Bowen, who shared the plunder, and whom they were supposed to have put out of the way, as he suddenly and mysteriously disappeared. But Stuart's dead body was found shortly afterwards under his dray's wheel in a creek, with his horses harnessed, on the way to Ravenswood.

APPENDIX I.

SHIPS THAT WENT UP THE COAST.

Besides the vessels which went up the Coast enumerated in Chapter I., the following are mentioned by Henry Stuart Russell in his *Genesis of Queensland*:

In May, 1803, H.M.S. "Britomart," Capt. Peach and four vessels started from Sydney to go through Torres Straits (p. 20). On 24th August, 1824, H.M.S. "Tamar," Capt. Sir Jas. Gorden Bremer, C.B., and the "Countess of Harcourt," Capt. Bunn, left Sydney for Port Essington, via Torres Straits. They were accompanied by the brig "Lady Nelson," 60 tons, which Russell refers to as the Tinder Box (p. 29). In September, 1838, H.M.S. "Alligator," Capt. Sir J. G. Bremer, and H.M.S. "Britomart," in command of Lieut. Owen Stanley (afterwards well-known for his explorations in New Guinea), started for Port Essington, via Torres Straits (p. 40). In the following year the cutter "American," bound from Moreton Bay to Port Essington, was wrecked at Cape York, and only a white woman saved by the Blacks (p. 45).

As regards the brig "Lady Nelson," which played such an important part in the exploration and navigation of the East Coast of Australia, she left Melville Island, North Australia, in 1824, in company with the schooner "Stedcombe," and according to G. W. Earl (*Voyage of the "Dourga,"* pp. 142, 228, London, 1840), both vessels were cut off and their crews murdered off the Island of Baba or Timor Laut.

APPENDIX II.

THE ASCENT OF MOUNT DALRYMPLE.

The Hon. H. S. Finch-Hatton
with Heliograph.

C. C. Rawson by the
old Flagstaff.

Fig. 45.—Summit of Mount Dalrymple,   From a Photograph
by P. T Porter, May, 1883.

The first attempt to ascend Mount Dalrymple was made 23rd July, 1877, by the
Hon. Henry S. Finch-Hatton (the present Earl of Winchilsea and Nottingham), R.
Pole-Carew (now General Sir Reginald Pole-Carew), D. H. Dalrymple now M.L.A.,
C. Martin (younger brother of Jim and Bob Martin, who afterwards went to South Africa
to a Bank), Harry Robinson (Overseer of Foulden), E. J. Welch, R.N., E. S. Rawson,
and C. C. Rawson.   This expedition was a failure and returned on the fourth day.
The members took a wrong spur, got up to a height of 3,800 feet and then perceived
the summit some three miles away, a gorge about 3,000 feet deep intervening.   Heavy
rain and shortness of provisions made further efforts impossible, especially as three
of the party were knocked up.

The second attempt and first successful ascent was made on 5th May, 1878,
by Henry S. Finch-Hatton, Frank Boyle and C. C. Rawson.   The following
are verbatim extracts from the diary of the last-named:—"May 2nd.   Henry
and I with Frank Boyle [brother-in-law of A. T. Ball] also Hector Cameron [both
stockmen at Mount Spencer] and a black boy, started to make another attempt
to get to the top of Mount Dalrymple.   Rode up Cattle Creek to the Pinnacle,
where we crossed and ran up a creek about three miles through two scrubs
and then camped.   May 3rd. Left Hector and boy with horses; Henry, Frank

and I humped our drums* and started up the mountain, two miles up the new creek (Finch-Hatton's), and took what we thought to be the leading spur. Began raining at 10-30 a.m. and kept it up. Could not get any look out from top of spur so camped under big boulder; very wet. May 4th. Tried all the spurs leading from our camp, but too thick to see anything. Clouds lifted at 1-30 p.m., and we saw 'The Gibber,'† got our bearings and started straight for the mountain. Camped on a saddle, very wet all day and night. May 5th. Sunday. Rained all night and very thick this morning. Henry and Frank climbed trees for bearings and again spotted 'The Gibber.' Started straight for the mountain, the summit of which we reached at noon. Too thick to see anything. Clouds lifted at 5 p.m., and we saw about the finest sight it was ever my lot to witness. Magnificent panorama for about an hour, when clouds settled down and rain came on again. Too wet and thick to send up rockets. Camped in a cave at back. Henry shot a turkey just as we got to the top which was very welcome, as we had only a small johnny cake left. I killed a seven-foot carpet snake on the very top, which was all we had for breakfast. May 6th. Put up a flagstaff with Henry's blanket on it, and started down the mountain at 8 a.m., got to our horse camp at 4-45 p.m. Left at 5 p.m., and got home [The Hollow] at 9 p.m., having been wet through since Friday at 10-30 a.m., and short of grub."

The second ascent of Mount Dalrymple took place in July, 1878. The party consisted of Henry S. Finch-Hatton (leader), J. Ewen Davidson, G. H. Maitland King (of Branscombe, and afterwards of Fryerne), A. H. Lloyd (Lloyd & Walker, Dumbleton), D. H. Dalrymple, Dick Mackenzie (who with his brother, James, owned Gairloch on the Herbert River), and E. S. Rawson. Finch-Hatton and Mackenzie camped a second night on the top to let off rockets, while the rest of the party returned to camp at foot, joining them the next morning at 10 o'clock. This party started on the 3rd July picking up the leading spur which starts at the junction of Finch-Hatton's and Rawson's creeks, about four miles up from the horse camp of the first expedition where there is a tree marked with a +. Their heliograph signals were seen distinctly from "The Hollow" and Mackay between 8-30 a.m. and 2 p.m., and their rockets and blue lights at 8 p.m.

The third ascent was made on May 20th, 1883, by Henry S. Finch-Hatton, P. Tindal Porter (Gov. Surveyor), and C. C. Rawson. They camped two nights on the summit, took four photos; fifteen feet of the flagstaff erected five years before were found to be still standing, and 35 new ferns were collected.

The fourth and last ascent was made on June 24th, 1884, by Henry S. Finch-Hatton, Dyson Lacy (of St. Helens), E. Lascelles, and C. C. Rawson, who all camped on the top for three nights.

"The mountain" writes C. C. Rawson to me, is entirely covered with dense vine scrub, and there are two kinds of tree ferns right up to the top. It is 4,250 feet high by aneroid, and there were no signs of it having been ascended by man before we went up; there were no traces of Blacks above the 2,000 feet line."

* To "hump one's drum" is to carry one's blanket on the back in a large roll like an elongated drum.

† "Gibber," *i.e.*, a large stone.

APPENDIX III.

THE ABORIGINES OF MACKAY.

Fig. 46.—Aborigines of Mackay. From a photograph, taken by Boag & Mills in 1872.

It is very doubtful whether the black human beings who were met with in this district by Captain Mackay and his successors, any more than the majority of the inhabitants of Australia when first seen by Europeans, were the aborigines of the continent.   There is very good reason for believing that their ancestors drove out a negroid race, which was the real aboriginal race, and that that negroid race was represented until the middle of last century by the Tasmanians.*   However, we have become so accustomed to calling the black Australians the aborigines that we may as well continue to do so here.

Of the aborigines in this district, very little has been recorded, and for that little we are indebted to George Bridgeman (the first Superintendent of Aborigines at Mackay, and brother of Frank Bridgeman), who supplied notes about

* See H. Ling Roth's "*Aborigines of Tasmania*," 2nd Ed., Halifax, 1899.

them to R. Brough Smythe for his work, *The Aborigines of Victoria* (Melbourne 1878). The most interesting feature in the life of these unhappy Australians was their tribal organisation.   Even up to thirty years ago students had hardly realised its importance in the history of the early development of mankind, and since that time in the Mackay district at any rate, the aborigines, if not all exterminated, have at least, through European influence, lost all knowledge of their old laws and customs.   But from what Bridgeman has related, it is clear that the Mackay aborigines belonged to the great Kamilaroi organisation.   He says:—

"All Blacks are divided into two classes, irrespective of tribe or locality.   These are Youngaroo and Wootaroo (end of each word sounded 'rue').   The Youngaroo are subdivided into Gurgela and Bembia, and the Wootaroo into Coobaroo and Woongo.   The first divisions have no feminine; the subdivisions have, namely, Coobaroon and Woongoon.   Every man, woman, and child necessarily belongs to one first division and one second.   Gurgela marries Coobaroon, and Bembia, Woongoon.   Children belong to the mothers' primary division, but to the other subdivision.   Thus Youngaroo-Gurgela marries Wootaroo-Coobaroon, and their children are Wootaroo-Woongo.

"Although on paper this looks rather complicated, it is, when understood, very simple.   The Blacks seem to have an idea that these classes are a universal law of nature, so they divide everything into them.   They tell you that alligators are Youngaroo, and kangaroos are Wootaroo—the sun is Youngaroo and the moon is Wootaroo; and so on with the constellations, with the trees, and with the plants. But even when one knows the language, it is hard to get information from this people, because they lack the power of concentrating and collecting their ideas, which is natural to educated people.

"On the system just described hinges all their ideas of relationship.   Their terms for father, mother, brother, sister, uncle, aunt, &c., &c., are by no means synonymous with ours, but convey different ideas.   From my long connection with the Blacks, they have given me a name and a grade amongst themselves, and there are many here who I do not suppose know my proper name.   I have several names, but the one I am usually called is *Goonurra*, which has no meaning—is only a name.   I am Youngaroo and Bembia, carrying out the former idea; and if I had children they would be Wootaroo and Coobaroo.   When a strange girl comes here I do not ask her name—that would be improper, according to the Blacks' ideas—nor can I ask what class she belongs to, but I say to another, " What am I to call her ? "   The answer may be (if she is Coobaroon) *Woolbrigan uno nulla*—" Daughter yours she. *Mollee dunilla indu*—" Mollee, say you ? "   *Mollee* being the term which all fathers call their daughters—daughter meaning any young woman belonging to the class which my daughter would belong to if I had one.   I give this example as the easiest way of conveying an idea of their system.   Blacks in their native state—that is before they pick up our manners and customs—never call each other by name. They always use a term of relationship, but use names, in speaking of another, in the third person."

Bridgeman once heard a funeral oration delivered over the grave of a man who had been a great warrior, which lasted more than an hour.   The corpse was borne on the shoulders of two men, who stood at the head of the grave.   During the discourse he observed that the orator spoke to the deceased as if he were still living and could hear his words.   Burial in the district in which Bridgeman lived is only a formal ceremony, and not an absolute disposal of the remains.   After lying in the ground for three months or more, the body is disinterred, the bones are cleaned and packed in a roll of pliable bark, the outside of which is painted and ornamented with strings of beads and the like. This, which is called *Ngobera*, is kept in the camp with the living. If a stranger who has known the deceased comes to the camp, the *Ngobera* is brought out towards evening, and he and some of the near relations of the dead person sit down by it, and wail and cut themselves for half-an-hour. Then it is handed to the stranger, who takes it with him and sleeps by the side of it, returning it in the morning to its proper custodian. Women and children who die, Bridgeman says, are usually burnt.

The following is Bridgeman's description of some implements, etc., of the Mackay Aborigines :—

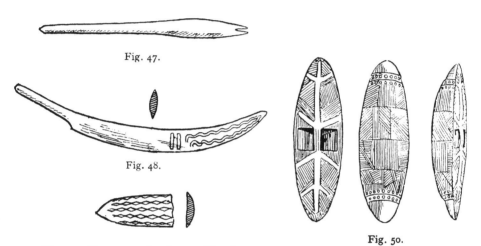

Fig. 47.

Fig. 48.

Fig. 49.—Boomerang, local name *Wongala*.

Fig. 50.

The weapon (Fig. 47), is a double-pointed *Nulla-Nulla*, called *Meero*. Rough instruments similar to this are used for killing game, but that here figured is employed only when fighting. It is either thrown at the enemy, or used to pierce him in close combat. The weight of this missile is twenty-four ounces.

The wooden sword [?] (Fig. 48) is two feet eleven inches in length, and rather more than two inches and three-quarters in breadth. It is coloured with a bright red pigment, and farther ornamented with rude serpentine streaks of white clay. It weighs forty one-ounces, is used with two hands to strike the back of an opponents neck and break it. Its name is *Bittergan*.

A shield (Fig. 50). The back, front, and sides are shown in the engraving. It is rudely but profusely ornamented, with shallow incised lines irregularly disposed, but so as to form a pattern. The two rows of shallow depressions marked with detached circles, at the top and bottom are coloured red. The spaces at the ends are painted white. The back is nearly flat, and the handle is cut out of the solid wood. A figure, perhaps that of some reptile, is drawn on it, and coloured white, and the spaces marked with incised lines are painted red. This shield is twenty inches and a quarter in length, and seven inches in breadth, and weighs only thirty-six ounces. The name of this shield is *Goolmarry*.

An ornament worn round the forehead, named *Ngungy-ngungy.* The shells, fragments of the nautilus, are ground into form and strung on a fine twine made of the fibre of some plant (Fig. 51). Larger pieces of shell, also of the nautilus,

Fig. 51.

Fig. 52.

are worn on the breast, suspended from the neck, and are called *Carr-e-la.* These are also strung on twine of the same kind as that used for the stringing of the smaller pieces (Fig. 52).

Fig. 53—Sketches of Canoes, Shields, Huts, &c., and figures of the Natives of the East Coast of New Holland, drawn by an artist (probably Reynolds, and not Buchan, to whom they are attributed) in Cook's Expedition, British Museum.

It is needless to say that the loin cloths and skirts as depicted in the illustration, (Fig. 46), are European innovations; originally all the clothing the people possessed was in the shape of opossum, or wallaby, skin mantles. Curiously enough, all the individuals represented in the photograph have *woolly* hair, but this is due to the mud, etc., with which they beplaster their heads. Their hair is wavy.

The first reservation for the aborigines was at Walkerston. They were occasionally employed by J. Ewen Davidson and other planters to weed and to do other light work on the sugar plantations, but neither their physique nor previous life fitted them for such occupation. At riding some became adepts.

The celebrated Godefroy Museum of Hamburg had a collector on the coast from 1863 to 1873, who made several ineffectual efforts to induce squatters to shoot an aboriginal, so that she could send the skeleton to the Museum! On one occasion she asked an officer of the Native Police what he would take to shoot so and so, pointing to one of the Native Black Troopers. She got no human skins nor skeletons from the Mackay District. Nevertheless the aborigines have received poor courtesy at our hands, and in extenuation of such treatment, a great deal has been said about their treachery and their bloodthirsty propensities. But we must remember that to the best of their very limited knowledge and ability they did what they could to defend *their* country and lives. We were the aggressors and have deprived them of both. It ems the unfortunate fate of the Australian aborigine that he must go down before the white man.

APPENDIX IV.

NOTES ON NATURAL HISTORY AND SPORT.

Mackay in my time, I am speaking of 24 to 30 years ago, presented an interesting and comparatively new field for those who delight in the study of wild life, but on the other hand there were few who had much leisure in a rising district to indulge in such a hobby. Before I lived in Mackay, the only one who appears to have taken any interest in field natural history was a German collector of Godefroy's, named Hermann Kuntzler, who seemed to have had an extraordinary talent for discovering caterpillars and grubs, and guarding them until they had developed into the perfect insect, when he captured them. Since I was there I believe the only residents to make any natural history investigations in the district have been the brothers Rowland E. and Gilbert Turner, formerly of The Ridges, Mackay. But it is my hope that the few notes here put together may to some extent at least induce others to take up the study.

Perhaps the point which strikes an observer most, throughout any investigation he may have time to make, is the adaptability, which a large portion of the smaller fauna exhibit towards the altered conditions, which have been brought about by the advent of the white man. In the case of many square miles of richly-timbered country being brought into cultivation, the larger fauna and the avi-fauna very soon disappear, while the smaller animals may still find refuge in the vegetation left on the outskirts of the cultivated area. This disappearance has been specially emphasized in Mackay by the destructiveness of the Kanakas, who, since 1866, have been in the habit of making Sunday hunting excursions, and never spared young or breeding individuals. But with regard to the narrow strips of dense semi-tropical growth, which were almost invariably to be found on the banks of some of the sluggish streams and on a good deal of the backwaters, their inhabitants, if at all specialised, must all have been swept away, for the white man sees no beauty in their homes, the luxuriant scrub, requiring the rich soil for his cultivation.

11

One asks as one does of the Mosquitoes : " What did this smaller fauna live upon before the advent of the European?" The various species of *Psocidæ*, which destroy any small specimens you may have gathered in your little leisure, or the silverfish, which swam in your cupboards and drawers, what did they live on, or the ants, scavengers and general robbers, what did they live on, before bread and sugar and jams were left at their disposal? What did the orange sucking moths suck before oranges were introduced? Where did the wasps nest before houses were built and land was fenced? Now they build on the walls, behind pictures and on the ironbark fences. The frogs and geckoes have practically become domestic animals outside the immediate township. Except to an amateur naturalist most of these have not much interest. But it is interesting to see a spider hanging by her thread and grabbing at a passing unwary fly. So too it is interesting to see a wasp bring pollen (?) to its larvæ, to see the latter pop up their heads on the arrival of the parent, eat their fill and sink down again in the cell. If a sunbird build on one's verandah, or a stray so-called opossum—a pretty docile little beast which on a first acquaintance will readily take food out of one's hand—pay a visit, most householders will not object. Of course, it took a little time for some of the fauna to adapt themselves, the moths lived on the pink berries of the *Eugenias* (scrub cherries they are called), and according to R. E. Turner's experience it took them some years to find out that the introduced oranges were good to suck. His experience with flying foxes and opossums was somewhat similar—it took them some years to discover the goodness of newly introduced cultivated plants.

That very shy animal the Echidna has been seen at St. Helens and Repulse Bay by J. Ewen Davidson, and the Platypus has been seen by Lord Winchilsea at Mount Spencer, in Denison Creek, and he tells me it is also tolerably common in Funnel Creek, which runs up to Bolingbroke Station. Both creeks are on the watershed of the Fitzroy River. It is *said* to have been seen in Black's Creek, Stockyard Creek and Cattle Creek, all of which run into the Pioneer River.

As already mentioned the Australian sunbird *Cinnyris frenatus* (S. Müll), often constructs its long hanging nest on verandahs or other sheltered places. According to R. E. Turner " The entrance is protected by a slight projecting roof. The birds become quite tame, one pair nested on my verandah for two years in succession; there did not seem to be ever more than two eggs. The female bird had a habit of flying into the rooms and sitting in front of a mirror twittering for ten minutes or a quarter of an hour. The male never came into the room, and was rather more shy than the female. The young birds when hatched remained about the garden for some months but went away for the nesting season."

Of the wild fowl on Spiller's lagoon, John Spiller writes me :—" The wild fowl shooting in the old days was particularly good, and big bags could have been made, there being hundreds of duck and other game birds on this lagoon. At first I used it as a larder, never having more than one shot, and always getting two birds ; the others were not much frightened, they would rise and pitch again about 50 or 60 yards away perfectly contented. I did not go in for big bags on this water, but always protected the birds, and finally allowed no shooting whatever. Besides Ducks and Geese, there were numbers of other birds, *i.e.*, Snipe, Plover, Egrets, Spoonbill Cranes, Giant Cranes, Native Companions and Pelicans, and many of the smaller birds, the Sandpiper in particular. I remember on one occasion several of the Pelicans walked up some 150 yards to a lawn in front of the house, making a pretty picture. I have seen as many as 200 Magpie Geese (*Anseranas semipalmata*) on this water and around the edges at once, and became so fond of them, not shooting them, that they got to know me and let me get well within shot of them. When they got out on to the lands they would let me ride quite close to them, whereas they would not allow a stranger to get anywhere near." It was a very pretty sight. Then there was the channel billed Cuckoo (*Scythrops novae hollandiae*) known locally as Spiller's Pigeon. Rare were the visits of Black Swan and of the beautiful Regent Bird (*Sericulus melinus*).

Fig. 54.—Spiller's Lagoon, Pioneer Estate. From a photograph by E. J. Welch*, taken about the end of the year 1875, when he was superintending the building of the Bridge across the Pioneer River at the Hermitage.

About 1898, when R. G. Turner sold the thick timber at the back of his property and it was cut down, about 20 Regent Birds settled in his garden, including 4 males, the rest being females and young. The Bustard (*Eupodotis australis*) is still met with across the range where not harassed.

This account of the existence of numerous wildfowl confirms Leichhardt in his remarks about the quantity of bird life as quoted above.

The Wedge Tailed Eagle (locally called the Eagle Hawk) used to be common. I obtained one young, about twelve months old, from Mount Spencer, and presented

* E. J. Welch was the fortunate member of the Burke and Wills Relief Expedition, who discovered King, the sole survivor of the ill-fated party (See E. Favenc, *Hist. Austral. Exploration*, Sydney, 1888). He is brother of Capt. David Welch, R.N., well-known in connection with His Majesty's yacht.

it in 1884 to the London Zoo, where it lived for ten years. It was very tame, was fond of being stroked, and allowed itself to be handled; it had a curious way of putting its beak sideways against my cheek, opening and closing the beak slightly and gently—a sort of side kissing. Of its nestings, Lord Winchilsea writes me:—"all I have seen nested in big gum or ironbark trees, usually some way up a hill, hanging over a steep gulley. The eggs almost exactly resembled those of the 'Golden Eagle' of the British Isles.

"The Fishing Eagle is a bird with grey wings and back, and a white breast, about the same size as the 'Sea Eagle' in this country. This bird lived principally on water fowl, such as coots, &c., and fish. It used to build in big gum trees near the water from which it obtained its food. The nest I took was built in a huge gum tree close to the margin of the lagoon in front of our house. The stem of the tree was perfectly smooth and straight, and about 7 feet in diameter, and fully 40 feet to the first branch. I induced a black fellow, by threats, persuasion, and bribes, to go up and let the young ones down with a string and basket. One of these subsequently died, but the other became quite tame and would sit on my knee to eat its fish or bird. Eventually Lady Winchilsea brought it home and presented it to the Zoo, where it lived for some years. It was rather a job to feed it on board, and pens of chickens and ducks had to be provided to keep it in fresh food on the journey."

Of the Duck Shooting, the Lord Winchilsea has specially prepared for me the following notes:—

"The best sport in the duck shooting line that I ever had was in Queensland, and it consisted entirely in 'driving.' This we used to do, either where several lagoons could be found in close proximity to one another, or on the Pioneer River. As an instance of the first form of sport, we will take the lagoon in the front of the Mount Spencer head station. This was a shallow lagoon, some four or five miles in total circumference, and shaped like a figure of eight. Each end consisted of a large shallow lagoon, in no place more than six or seven feet deep, thickly fringed with reeds, and almost entirely overgrown with blue water-lilies. Both these ends in severe droughts become quite dry, but, in an average ordinary dry season, they remained full of water for some time after the neighbouring creeks and water-holes were practically dried up. At this time of the year ducks of every description, at all times pretty numerous, collected in large quantities on the lagoon, and this was the time we used to choose for shooting. The two ends of the lagoon were connected at their junction by a long deep water-hole about 30 yards in width, and the tall gum trees which surrounded the lagoon came together at this point to within a distance of about 150 yards. Across this narrow neck ran the posts and rails of different paddock fences, and behind these fences we posted three or four guns. One or two "black fellows" in canoes then advanced on one end of the lagoon and put up the ducks, which immediately made their way over the heads of the guns to the other end. When everything that could possibly be induced to fly had left this end of the lagoon, the beaters went round to the other end and drove back as many of the ducks as would face the guns again, together with those which belonged to that part of the water. All sorts of ducks, black ducks, wood ducks, widgeon, teal, shovellers, two sorts of whistlers, and pigmy geese (both the common and painted varieties), kept rocketing over our heads in mobs of from two or three to 50 or 60 for the greater part of the afternoon, usually at a height from which it took a good gun to bring them down. As a rule Queensland gunners in those days were not very much accustomed to shooting driven birds, otherwise very big bags would have been obtained. The heaviest that I recollect was 118 birds in one afternoon to three guns.

"This was on the 4th July, 1888, when I with L. K. Rice bagged 111 birds, and another man 7—total 118. The bag consisted of 89 black duck, 13 widgeon, 10 teal, 4 pigmies,* and 2 wood duck; no whistlers. Other good records are—52 birds, 8th November, 1883, C. C. Rawson, G. H. M. King, and H. S. Finch-Hatton; 84 on 5th July, 1884, E. G. Lascelles, H. S. Finch-Hatton, and A. Finch-Hatton: this bag consisted of 42 black duck, 23 widgeon, 3 teal, 1 whistler, 1 shoveller, 10 pigmies, 2 coots, and 2 quail; 68 on 21st July, 1887, J. Ewen Davidson, G. H. M. King, Basil Brooke, L. K. Rice, H. S. Finch-Fitton, and A. E. Boyle; 54 on 9th December, 1887, H. S. Finch-Hatton alone, 30 black duck, 9 wood duck, 3 whistlers, and 7 pigmies, exclusive 5 lost, with a total expenditure of 80 cartridges, from 3—6 p.m.

"On the Pioneer River the sport was even better. This river is one of those that flow direct to the sea from the coast range, and, in consequence, is in contradistinction to the greater number of rivers which flow behind the coast range, a constant-running stream with a perennial supply of beautiful clear water. In the dry time of the year when water holes, lagoons and smaller creeks all over the country are running dry, ducks come down to the river in great quantities. The plan of campaign was for four or five guns to get on their horses and proceed to a given spot on the river where the stream was broken up into islands and the guns could be strung across. Two beaters, usually "black fellows," then drove a reach of the river from one to two miles in length, over the heads of the guns, always driving up stream, as we found that ducks, when put up, invariably flew in this direction. The river flowed between banks which were from 100 to 250 yards apart, the banks themselves being very steep, about 80ft. high, and clothed in many places with dense jungle, and in all other parts with open forest. The birds used to hug the line of the river, flying about level with the tops of the trees, and came in an almost unbroken succession of mobs of from two or three to twenty or thirty at a time. When the drive was over, the guns would jump on to their horses and canter on to the next stand, where the operation was repeated until darkness put an end to the sport.

"Records:—October 11th, 1883, in Five Drives (1) Jacks Camp to McGregors Creek, (2) Weaners Crossing, (3) Hamilton Pool Rocks, (4) Cattle Creek, (5) Mia Mia. Five guns and one beater. Result: 43 ducks. October 12th, 1883, in Six Drives (1) Pearl Flat to bottom of Pigmy Hole, (2) Mia Mia, (3) Cattle Creek, (4) Nith Hole, top end, (5) Jacks Camp to McGregors Creek and (6) Weaners Crossing. Five guns and one beater. Result: 33 ducks and 2 pigmies. Hardly anything but black duck and a few widgeon. Drought of four months broke up on 11th, so it was well timed. But Ducks not so plentiful as they were three or four years ago and fly very high.

"I think I have assisted at almost all sorts of driving, from partridge driving in England to *Capercaillie* driving in Norway, and if I were given my choice of the lot, I would choose a day's duck driving on the Pioneer River before any of them."

Crocodiles were once very numerous. In Fig. 55 is an illustration from a photograph taken by E. S. Rawson, of a crocodile shot in 1871, on the banks of the Pioneer River, near Branscombe, by G. N. Marten. Length, 15ft. 3in.; girth, 6ft. 6in.

---

* Pigmies are pigmy geese, beautiful little birds, about the size of a teal. They generally flew very low and very fast, as a rule three or four of them in a mob.

It should be noted that, although these reptiles are almost invariably spoken of as alligators, correctly speaking, they should be called crocodiles, Mr. Boulenger, F.R.S., of the British Museum, having identified the above for me as *Crocodilus porosus*.* As they have now wholly disappeared from the Pioneer River, some account of them may not be out of place here, and I therefore subjoin what E. B. Kennedy says of them in his interesting little book, *Four Years in Queensland*, London, 1870, adding other notes about them :—

"The squatters cannot keep a cattle dog, and the planters are always losing their setters and kangaroo hounds. These dogs, I am convinced from my own observations, are generally taken in small lagoons, within a mile or so of the river proper : for, as more game abounds about the lagoons than on the river bank, the dogs are taken there for shooting, &c., and when swimming about to cool themselves they are seized. A gentleman was out duck shooting on a lagoon within a mile of his house, when walking through some long reeds he suddenly descried what appeared to be a scrub-turkey's (*Talegalla*) nest ; he was preparing for some sport, when his setter, who had

Fig. 55.—*Crocodilus porosus*.

been snuffing about the supposed bird's nest, ventured near some of the long reeds and was suddenly snapped at by an alligator ; the dog gave a yell and a bound, and escaped its formidable enemy, but the sportsman was now within five feet of the alligator, and face to face with him. He drew the shot from both barrels, and rammed down a couple of bullets, tearing off a piece of his shirt to use as a patch, and thereby ensuring a tight fit, but never taking his eyes off the alligator who lay perfectly motionless. He told us afterwards that his hands shook so much from excitement that he could scarcely load. He must, however, have regained his coolness very quickly, for he placed the ball so truly through the beast's eye that its eyelid was not injured ; it then rushed past him, he giving it a second ball in the teeth *en passant*, and buried its head in a tuft of grass, giving vent to a hissing sound. S——* then cooey'd for assistance, and a rifle was brought, but the alligator was dead. It only measured nine feet, but judging by its teeth, which were black and decayed, like those of an old dog, it could not have been young ; it had lost a portion of its near fore leg. There were two well-trodden tracks between the nest and the water, the water being a small deep lagoon about 30 yards from the nest, and one of a long chain of lagoons ; there was also a circle of about 15 feet in diameter trodden evenly round the nest, as though an old treadmill horse had been at work there ; the nest itself was made of grass and fine sticks in short pieces, and contained 64 eggs in different layers. This alligator was, no doubt, the female guarding her nest. The

* " Both crocodiles and alligators are linked so closely together that anatomy is somewhat hard put to it to separate them by any than the most trivial characters."—F. E. Beddard, F.R.S., *Nat. Hist. in Zool. Gardens.* Lond., 1905.

eggs seem to be prodigious in number,† but we are told that quantities of the young are eaten by the bull alligators as soon as they are hatched by the heat of the sun. The eggs are about the size of a turkey's, but not the same shape, being equal in size at both ends. They are of a dirty white, with tiny dents in them, and a little black spot every here and there, giving them rather the appearance of some kinds of marble. They are of an elastic nature when full, and will *give* on being pushed. They *crack* easily, but always hold together, for there is a tough skin underneath the shell; we blew young alligators out of some of them. When fresh, the eggs are not bad eating.

"Some South Sea Islanders, employed on one of the plantations, told us that they had run a calf belonging to their master, into the water. Two alligators shoved off, if I may so express it, from the back of the lagoon towards it; but the Islanders swam in, rescued the calf, and when asked if they were not afraid, said, they found they could swim faster than the alligators, and I quite believe their story.‡ The way that these reptiles catch most of their victims is by quietly swimming along the edge of the lagoons or rivers by night; they glide quite under the bank, keeping their two legs next to it, flush with their bodies, and thus are enabled to seize any unlucky calf or wallaby that comes down to drink. I have often found the undigested feet of both in their stomachs, also the bills of water birds. They seem to fight very much, and most of them are minus one fore foot, or bear marks of teeth on their bodies. They are great cowards out of the water, and very difficult to stalk, in fact much harder than a duck, that is to say to approach quite close to; shoes must be taken off and great patience exercised. The crocodile of the Nile always has a bird near him, who wakes him at the approach of danger; but the Queensland alligator has no such sentry, and consequently is nearly always on the look out. Whenever I have shot at alligators and missed them, I have noticed that they invariably, after having plunged into the water, come to the surface for a few seconds, usually only showing their heads; they then, however, disappear for hours. In taking aim, the best spot to fire at is behind and a little below the jaw; it is very hard to kill one outright. They so often, though mortally wounded, manage to struggle into the water. One was shot with a long Enfield at about fifty yards; the ball entered just behind the jaw, and the blood spouted out in one thick stream, he had about six yards to get to the water; he accomplished five, and died just on the brink. Though the hide is very thick, a ball will, most certainly, pierce it, but it is not likely to touch a vital part.

"It was a great joke with two of us that, in skinning an alligator, we could not find any heart, though it is to be supposed that he had one in common with every other animal, yet, all we could find was a small piece of tough looking substance in that part of the body where this important organ is supposed to exist.

"The best time for finding alligators out basking is in the winter months—May, June and July—for then the water is cold, and they lie out on the banks during the warmest part of the day. A very favourite haunt is where a small creek empties itself into the river; at the junction of the two there is usually a corner of sand backed

---

* This was John Spiller.

† C. C. Rawson informs me that nests have been found on the banks of the Pioneer containing from 45 to 72 eggs.

‡ In January, 1872, a Kanaka was devoured by an alligator on the Burdekin River. In 1878, when the "Llewellyn" surveying vessel was off Flat Top, a Kanaka deliberately jumped on top of a shark and drove it away.

by a few reeds; if you do not find one there, look for his tracks, both under the water at the edge, and on the land, for he leaves the impression of his big claws and tail. When the alligator is not molested, he will come out day after day in exactly the same spot, and it is curious to see the track he leaves; it is in the shape of a horse-shoe, the portions not joined being, of course, the water; so that he evidently creeps out, basks, and when he has stayed long enough, turns leisurely round, and back to the water.

"Owing to floods, these sand banks are left, by the ebbing of the waters, in large ribs or ridges, and by crawling along on one's stomach, one may get within a few yards of the alligator, having first taken the bearings from some neighbouring high ground. When you suppose you are near enough, as you raise your head, keep your rifle at your shoulder, at the '*present*,' for the probability is that he will be off at almost the first movement you make. Some have an idea that he can glide into the water without making any commotion in it whatever; the shape of his body certainly allows him to make less than any other animal, but there are always signs left on the surface, and in shallow water he is a most clumsy beast, stirring up the mud with his legs and tail.

"I recollect one who had got into a narrow channel in about three feet of water, being chased by two men with stockwhips; his pursuers were gaining upon him, and he was doing his best, evidently in a dreadful fright, when he suddenly disappeared in a deep hole at the end of the channel."

Another crocodile's nest was described to me by J. Ewen Davidson: It was half way between Pleystone and Balnagowan on the south bank of the Pioneer River (exposed to the northern sun) about 30 feet from the water, in a bit of wet ground on the bank caused by the outbreak of a small spring. The nest was of rotten grass, small sticks and leaves, and was kept moist by the water from the spring. The eggs were just visible, being lightly covered with leaves. The combination of hot sun and decaying vegetation gave the heat necessary for hatching. It has been said that in ordinary cases the nest is sufficiently near the water for the crocodile to splash water with its tail, at night, over the rubbish, and in one instance some people in a boat camped near, heard the splashing and found the nest next day, but this was on the Mosman River, further north.

John Spiller, who shot nine crocodiles, writes me he did not think it much sport. They used to come up to the cattle paddock at the Pioneer in search of calves, so he had to shoot them. Charles E. Romilly (A. Hewitt's partner at Pleystone) informs me he shot 27 in the reaches from the Washpool past Pleystone to the Hollow.

In the *British Museum (Natural History) Guide to the Gallery of Reptilia and Amphibia*, London, 1906, it is stated that crocodiles "generally seize their victims (other than human beings) by the nose when drinking." This, however, refers to the Indian species, for the Mackay crocodiles as we have seen above used to come out into the paddocks to attack the calves, although generally it was when animals came down to the water to drink, or to cross, that the crocodiles attacked them. Spiller tells me the crocodiles used to wait for their victims at the edge of the water their tails lying on the bank and whilst the animal is drinking they sweep it into the water, then seize it and take it under. The Rawsons once had a horse's cheek laid open with a clean cut like a knife by a crocodile, which may have been done with claws or teeth as the horse was drinking; the other cheek had slight scratches only. It had not been caught by the snout. Once they had a horse dragged down bodily while being towed across, behind a boat in the pool under 'The Nyth.' R. K. Graham, of St. Helens was once seized by the foot by the mouth of a crocodile whilst crossing a flooded creek. The crocodile held on till he nearly got across the river. But for the stirrup iron, held up by the stirrup leather, which prevented the jaws closing, his foot would have been torn off; as it was, his boot was cut as with a knife, and the stirrup iron so compressed that he could hardly get his foot out. I remember a journeyman saddler who was humping his drum* from Port Curtis along the coast nearly coming to grief through a crocodile's attack. It was, I believe, at Baker's Creek, which he wished to cross at its mouth late in the afternoon, when he was caught by the tide. Throwing off his 'drum' he pushed it in front of him and made for what he thought was a large log floating up. But he had hardly realised his mistake when the brute dashed noisily at him, snapped at the blanket and tore swiftly off with it. He did not give the crocodile time to realise that it too had made a mistake! H. M. Finlayson, of Port Newry, had a very narrow escape in crossing a creek, near Cape Hilsborough; the crocodile seized the horse by the shoulder, ripping the flesh from the bone. G. H. M. King once saw a crocodile rush splashing across the river after one of his dogs, that was swimming near the opposite bank. Crocodiles were found so far up the Pioneer as Black's and Cattle Creeks, that is close on 26 miles up.

The crocodiles, when basking on the sand, generally chose positions which are more or less sheltered, they kept mostly on the flat and did not expose themselves on the rocks, as they are not infrequently depicted in book illustrations (*see Living Animals of the World*, 1st Ed., London, II., p. 549). The position of their eyes is such as to enable them to look upward, rather than downward, which is probably a consequence of their having to look for their prey on the water level or above it. Hence, whatever crocodiles may do in captivity, in the wild state they do not rise and expose themselves above water level more than is necessary.

As regards that ever feared reptile the snake, you may be having an afternoon nap, and, rousing, may find a curious deep orange-coloured zig-zag thing with a flickering split tongue swaying over your head—when in all probability you will get up somewhat quicker than you had intended doing. But such visitors are rare, and cases of snake bite are not often heard of, and only in two cases did I assure myself of the correctness of snakes making aggressive attacks. Generally they are in greater haste to get away than we are. During thirty-four years residence at Mackay, out of a large number of Kanaka labourers (going into the thousands) J. Ewen Davidson only had three bitten by snakes, and that was in the cane fields when the 'boys' were *trashing*, and the snakes, not being able to escape, attacked them. But it must not be thought snakes have no enemies beyond human beings. I remember once riding leisurely home on the Farleigh Road, when I heard a slight rustling in the grass, and getting off my horse observed a fight between an agamid lizard (popularly called an iguano) and a *Dipsadomorphus fuscus*, the well-known copper coloured snake of the district. The snake was caught not far from the head and was being shaken as a rat is by a terrier. It made no attempt to bite nor to crush its antagonist, but appeared as a wriggling, almost spiral, coil, such as snakes do not usually assume, though often so depicted. As soon as the lizard espied me it went off, so I measured the dying

---

* This man was not a "Sundowner" (one who arrives at a station just in time to share the evening meal, and is off again in the morning without working it out) but a steady man who went the round of the stations, and some of the plantations, repairing harness, etc.

snake which was 3 ft. 7 in. long; the length of its enemy being about 2 ft. 6 in. Once on cutting open an agama I found portions of a snake inside.

Other enemies of the snakes are the so-called Laughing Jackass (*Dacelo gigas*). It is generally said that this kingfisher kills its prey by letting it drop a few times on the ground, and Prof. R. Semon* repeats this statement without saying that he actually saw a snake so killed. The only time I saw this bird with a snake, it had hold of the snake in its beak, and was banging the snake's head against a tree branch, the rest of the snake's body hanging down fairly limply. J. Ewen Davidson's experience in this matter was the same as mine. Since the introduction of the cat snakes have made the acquaintance of a new enemy, which, while it frequently kills them, is not known to eat them.

Snakes are amongst the quietest of animals in their movements. I once saw a *Tropidonotus picturatus* on the watch for tadpoles. The snake lay perfectly still in a small pool of water, and every now and then made a dart at the tadpoles. I remember one beautifully quiet Sunday morning, when living at Miclere, enjoying the lovely view of the sea from that height, when I was suddenly aroused by a terrible croaking on the upper side of the wooden ceiling of my room, and at the same moment but not before I heard the heavy thuds of the house-frogs (*Hyla cærulea*) hurrying apparently in all directions. On clambering up I found a large black snake (*Hoplocephalus*) had caught a frog by the side of the snout. The frog was roaring lustily, and his mates, in that peculiar swelled attitude they adopt when angered, were hopping away as fast as they could. Until the wretched frog was caught and consequently began to bellow, not one of the frogs had appeared to budge any more than they would do, if disturbed by any human beings. The snake seemed to move his jaws sideways until he got his victim facing him, never letting go, and then, although the wretched frog kept on bellowing, he gradually drew it down alive, and it was choked as it went down. There was no attempt at enfolding the frog in his coils as the carpet snake does a rat and so strangle it. If the poison fangs were brought into requisition, the frog was swallowed before the poison could have acted.

On one occasion I saw a couple of black snakes (probably a species of *Hoplocephalus*) standing up above the grass in a paddock apparently slightly intertwined, their bodies being more or less in a wavy position, their necks somewhat arched so that their heads were somewhat vertically inclined and facing each other. There was a slight swaying movement, and then they appeared to drop away separately. I had not seen them rise, nor could I see the lower part of their bodies owing to the intervening grass. As these snakes have some affinities with the cobra it is more than likely that this pair were in the act of rutting. J. Ewen Davidson once saw two snakes amongst some boulders in the dry portion of the river bed rearing up 3 or 4 feet from the sand, with their heads about 6 inches apart, but their lower lengths were not visible owing to the stones or brushwood. They were either playing or in the act. They were, however, a black and a brown snake, which the introduced Malay labourers say are male and female. The snakes were in the position named about five minutes when Davidson's companion shot them. They measured over 10 feet in length.

Carpet Snakes (*Python spilotes*) make very good pets, but are mostly nocturnal in their habits. I had one big vicious one—perhaps the loss of an eye long previous to

---

* *In the Australian Bush*, London, 1899, p. 81. This is a useful work where the Author gives his own experiences and does not rely upon hearsay evidence. It can be well recommended to all lovers of field natural history in Queensland, who will find much to delight them in it.

his capture made him so—10½ feet long. I never could do anything with him. But another, 6½ feet long, which at first was inclined to be vicious and would snap at any one approaching his cage, afterwards became very tame and appeared to enjoy being handled. In very hot dry weather he liked lying in the water, and in the cold months (July and August) he hid under his blanket. At first I gave him frogs to eat, the common Queensland house frogs, if I may so name them (*H. cærulea*), but he took no notice of them; they squatted comfortably on him, and unless they disturbed him by moving he did not seem to mind. A frill lizard, another small agama, various small lizards, a duck, a small parrot, a small fowl, and chickens were placed in his cage from time to time, but remaining unnoticed were severally removed after a few days, one fowl being squashed by being caught between his folds as he uncoiled himself. On the 16th March, 1883, I gave him a snake (*Dipsadomorphus fuscus*) about 15ins. long, which disappeared on the 29th. Whether the carpet snake swallowed him I could not say, but there did not seem to be any possibility of escape for the small snake, as the cage was a large, specially built, tight fitting wooden box, with glass sliding door and perforated zinc ventilator, all well fitted together by a cabinet maker, kept under lock and key. On May 12th, 1883, I gave him a mouse which I found dead on the 14th. On the 25th he was given a full grown rat. He roused to this at once and caught it by the snout. The rat gave one squeal and all was over—really a gunshot could not have done the work quicker. The act of catching and coiling round the rat seemed done instantaneously together, and his victim was crushed. Unfortunately he was disturbed and did not swallow the rat. On 5th September I put a rat into the cage (a new one with wired front). The rat showed no sign of fear at sight of the snake—it went up to the snake, smelt him at various parts, and beyond seeing me through the wires it appeared quite contented and happy, and began to look for food, or appeared to be doing so. The snake soon became alive to the fact that a breakfast was awaiting him, caught it in a trice, swallowed it and prepared to rest in elongated coils, as he always did when he had a meal, and not in the more or less circular coils, as he did, when he had an empty stomach. On September 21st, 1883, he had another rat, but, after three vain attempts to catch it, he caught it by the loin, and altogether seemed to manage very badly, and the rat tried to bite him, but did not succeed. Twenty-seven minutes after capture all but the rat's tail had disappeared. The next morning he had another rat; this also he caught clumsily, and not having caught it by the head seemed to have some difficulty in satisfying himself where that was. In 64 minntes from the time of capture the rat had completely disappeared, the jaws had set themselves again and he commenced to settle down. On 5th October I gave him three mice, he swallowed one, and the other two I let out next morning, as their puny caperings appeared to irritate him. He evidently only killed when he wanted something to eat. On November 2nd, 1883, I gave him a rat which he disposed of as follows: he caught it at 11-14 a.m., at 11-18½ he uncoiled and started on the head at once, at 11-25½ the first shoulder was down, and at 11-37½ the tail had disappeared. The time occupied was his record, being 23½ minutes. I then gave him another rat, but this fellow stood up to fight and attacked the snake, and, although its teeth did not appear to harm him, they annoyed him. The snake made several ineffectual darts at the rat but failed, not seeming to *see* where the rat was as he always struck the air. So I removed the rat. The snake was evidently getting ready for his change, and on 29th November he shed his skin, rubbing it off on the branches in his cage, which were left covered with pieces of slough. He was now beautiful to look at, very lively, and to stroke him was like feeling velvet.   On the 6th October he had thrown up a quantity of dark grey hairy matter, with a strong ammoniacal odour.*   Its digestion was evidently slow, as from the date of capture, 12th December, 1882, to 22nd March, 1883, a hundred days, it passed nothing.   The dissolved bones of his food were also passed separately.

When kept in a well-aired cage, which was carefully cleaned, there was practically no odour at all, but when kept in a glass-fronted box the odour was pungent and unpleasant, and hung about a long time.

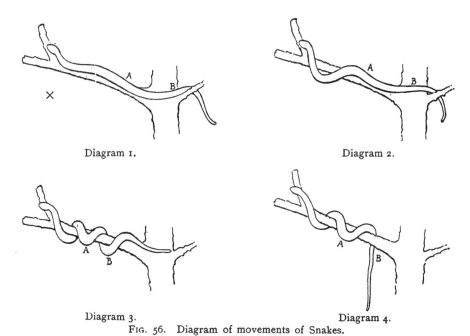

Diagram 1.   Diagram 2.

Diagram 3.   Diagram 4.

Fig. 56.   Diagram of movements of Snakes.

(1) Moving slowly on belly along a branch.   (2) Commencing the loop.   (3) The loop round the branch.   (4) The snake coiled round the branch.

When he wished to catch a rat he just brought his head closer to his victim, kept it steadily poised, with closed mouth for less than a minute, before striking.   The strike was made so quickly that I could not always be certain that I saw his mouth open, although I occasionally saw a large bluish-red gape.   To understand the lightening like rapidity with which a snake gets round his prey is not quite clear at first.   It is obvious that having got hold of his victim by his teeth he cannot coil himself from his head downwards into the form of a spiral wire spring,† nor does he do so, in fact that is a position very rarely assumed.   He must bring some other part of his body into play, and this is what he actually does, although it is not easily seen how he does it.   He

* An Indian (?) python I afterwards kept turned its neck upwards and top of head downwards when it threw up such matter.

† As above-mentioned, it is very rare that a snake assumes the form of a spiral spring, and should not be so drawn.   Unfortunately, Semon figures a *Pseudechis porphyriacus* in such a position. But his illustration is copied (unacknowledged) from Krefft's well-known work, and is evidently a squeezed up spirit specimen.

makes loops of his body, and by pushing separate loops round, forward and backward, he gets round his prey. When he wished to get round a branch of a tree for instance he did not wind round it head first, but fixing himself at some point × (see first diagram, Fig. 56) he gradually moved his ribs towards this point, so that this part of his body had the appearance of hanging down loosely, forming an incipient loop (second diagram). As this loop increased (it was kept close to the branch all the while) it was pushed round underneath the branch, and emerged on top again (see third diagram) where the portion of his body marked A had been round the branch, and was now on top but more forward. Then he would, perhaps, swing his tail over, or not (see fourth diagram). But in the meanwhile, most probably he would also be making another loop to go round the branch the other way. And it is this facility for making the loops either way, or both ways, that enables him to get round his victim so quickly.

It is strange he would not touch the birds, for in freedom carpet snakes have often been known to destroy fowls, and a friend of mine caught a carpet snake which had just killed five young chickens and was trying to capture the hen. Later on I put several other snakes, all of the same species, into his cage, and it was very funny at times to see the unheeded rats lying comfortably on top of the snakes, for the snakes often left them several days untouched.

Frog life is very pronounced at Mackay, the commonest frog *H. cærulea*, which by the bye is only blue in spirits, becoming in fact a nuisance in the houses, whither it is largely attracted by the moths and flies, drawn to the lamps at night, and the so-called black beetles, which congregate in and under human habitations. The frogs are to be found at all times. In the dry season hugging the water decanters, in the cold weather behind books, between the walls, and in the wet season, especially at night, they are all over the house, flopping about noisily and getting in your way when you are about. They will "go" for anything that moves—a bit of paper moved by the wind, or even a stud tied to a piece of thread and drawn along near them, "going" for it two, and even, three times before they discover it is not edible. They soon become tame and if fed at a certain spot, such as the corner of a table, will afterwards regularly visit that spot. On moonlight nights the croaking of the frogs is more than deafening; not the least noisy, in the day time also, is a beautiful little fellow known as *H. gracilenta*, which is to be found on the under surface of the leaves of the bushes. Then there is the toad-like *Chiroleptes australis*, which is said to wail like a child, but which sound I have not been able to distinguish. They all have different notes, which with the rising European population are translated into "quart pot" and such like words. Like everywhere else frogs have no end of enemies. Besides snakes and agamidæ, the rats are decidedly their enemies, and I have more than once heard the common house frog croaking in agony, and, on coming up, found one of its limbs bleeding, I afterwards found the wound was caused by rats—having come across a rat in the act. The latter catch the frog and apparently suck the blood, but do not I think eat any of the flesh, as I never found a frog so attacked on which the flesh had been destroyed. The mantis is another enemy. A friend of mine, W. Price Fletcher, once saw a mantis, about 5 inches long, which had hold of a small green frog, about 2 inches long; it held the frog with one claw across its neck so that the frog could not move, and the mantis was chewing, and did chew off, the hind leg, the blood flowing profusely. This was however at Rockhampton. At Lake Elphinstone I once found a small frog (*H. rubella*) in the house in a very exhausted condition; on examination a large leech was found on its tongue. The frog, with leech attached, is now in the Brit. Museum (Nat. Hist).

The frogs sent by me to the British Museum from Mackay were—

Limnodynastes peronii (L. lineatus of De Vis).
    ,,   *ornatus.*
    ,,   *dorsalis.*
    ,,   *olivaceus,* a new species; *Proc. Lin. Soc., N.S. Wales,*
        VOL. IX., 1884, p. 66.
Hyla   nasuta.
    ,,   *rubella.*
    ,,   *gracilenta.*
    ,,   *leseurii.*
    ,,   *cærulea.*
    ,,   *peronii (H. rothii of De Vis).*

Of fishing, the largest catch of Palmer (*Lates calcarifer*) ever made with one rod in the Pioneer was by G. H. M. King. There were 21 landed, weighing altogether 130 lbs. when home was reached (which means a tolerable loss). The largest 18 lbs., and the smallest 2¾ lbs. The fishing was from about 1 to 6 p.m. It is said that the heaviest fish caught in the Pioneer was 25 lbs. in weight with phantom minnow; but in the Fitzoy River much heavier ones have been caught in the net. At Foulden Crossing, Pioneer River, with seine net with two hands on, Oct. 17th, 1883, 53 Mullet, 3 Whiting, 3 Bream (some mullet 2½ lbs. weight) were caught. A sort of perch (*Therapon argentius*) I found in Lake Elphinstone, and I also found it in a pool not far from Mt. Gotthard.

Some of the notes on the habits of various wasps, which I made at Mackay, were considered of sufficient interest to be read before one of the meetings of the Fellows of the Linnean Society (London), and to be published in their Journal. At that time, however, the Australian Hymenoptera Aculeata had not been sufficiently worked out, and this, together with the fact that in the course of twenty-three years some of the names given have been superseded, I have thought it useful to my readers to have the names revised, and this Rowland E. Turner kindly undertook to do for me. In pursuing the paper here reprinted the reader will kindly note therefore that

Pelopæus formosus   is now substituted for   *P. lætus.*
Pison vestitum   ,,   ,,   ,,   *Pison spinolæ,*
Bembex palmata   ,,   ,,   ,,   *Bembex tridentifer,*
Meranoplus hirsutus,   ,,   ,,   ,,   *Meranoplus dimidiatus,*
Iridomyrex rufoniger,   ,,   ,,   ,,   *Formica rufoniger,*
Euponera lutea   ,,   ,,   ,,   *Ectatamma diminuta,*

To assist those who, on any part of the coast, may wish to continue the studies, I give illustrations of the wasps and ants, the habits of which are described.

The corrected Paper reads as follows:—

Notes on the Habits of some Australian Hymenoptera Aculeata. By HENRY LING ROTH. (Communicated by Sir J. LUBBOCK, Bart., Pres. Linn. Soc.)*

[MR. ROTH has recently transmitted to the British Museum, through Sir John Lubbock, a series of Ants and other Hymenoptera from Mackay, Queensland. By Mr. Roth's desire, I have selected such of his accompanying observations as appear to be of sufficient interest for publication, and have added the correct names of the

---

* Extracted from the *Linnean Society's Journal—Zoology, vol. xviii.*
[Read 20th November, 1884.]

Fig. 57.—Pelopœus formosus.
Smith.

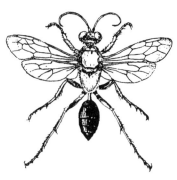

Fig. 58.—Sphex ephippium.
Sm.

Fig. 59.—Pison perplexum.
Sm.

Fig. 60.—Bembex
palmata. *Sm.*

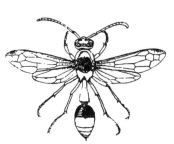

Fig. 61.—Eumenes Latreillei.
Sauss.

Fig. 62.—Apisba splendida.
Guérin.

Fig. 63.—Rhynchium
Rothi, sp. n.

Fig. 64.—Odynerus
bicolor.
Sauss.

Fig. 65.—Polistes
Bernardii.
Le Guillou.

Fig. 66,—Meranoplus
hirsutus. *Mayr.*
Sm.

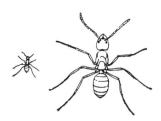

Fig. 67.—Iridomyrex rufoniger.
Lowne.

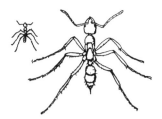

Fig. 68.—Euponera lutea.
Mayr.

Fig. 69.—Œcophylla
virescens.
Fab.

species.   I have also described a species of *Rhynchium* which seems to be new.—
W. F. Kirby.]

FOSSORES.
SPHEGIDÆ.

PELOPŒUS FORMOSUS, *Smith.*

These Wasps are exceedingly common.   When living in the country, it is very
difficult to keep them out of the house.   They build their nest anywhere and everywhere—on the walls, ceilings, on the legs of chairs, under the table, in crevices,
cupboards, in vases, between pictures and the walls, in the roof, once in a pipe (12th
Nov., 1883), and even on curtains.

They construct their nests very differently from *Eumenes Latreillei* (*vide infrà*,
Fig. 71).   Having chosen a desirable spot, they go in search of the necessary mud.
This they obtain from the moist or wet soil on the margin of creeks or puddles.
Having scraped enough particles together and made them up into a ball about the
size of their thorax, they carry it away and begin building.   The marks of the layers
of mud are very distinctly visible.   When the site chosen is not a very good one, as
for instance between a picture and the wall, these cells are sometimes flattened out in
course of construction, as shown in the accompanying Figs. 70—*a-e.*   I may here remark
that the layers of mud are not very distinctly shown in this figure, in consequence of
the wasp having been unable to obtain sufficiently dry mud, owing to the prevailing
wet weather, and the layers therefore run into one another.   When the mud is very
wet the wasp drops a quantity, and the ground below which she is building is
frequently covered with the fallen particles.

In her flight she stridulates very like a bee, but with a much deeper tone.   As
soon, however, as she has settled to work either in collecting mud or in the actual
construction of her nest, she produces quite a different sound.   It has now an
exceedingly high pitch; and from my observations of the wasp at work, I believe it
is the result of the vertical motion of the abdomen from the pedicle.

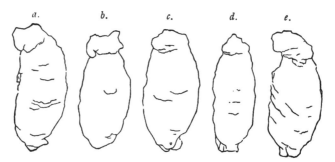

Fig. 70.—*a–e.*   Outlines, nests of *Pelopæus formosus,* nat. size.

The work which the wasp undertakes in building her nest may be judged from
the number of times she takes to go to and from the wet earth.   On Oct. 13th, 1883,
I timed a wasp at her work.   In the course of 22 minutes she fetched mud at a
distance of 5 yards; 13 times at the following intervals—at $14\frac{1}{2}$, $12\frac{1}{2}$, $10\frac{3}{4}$, $9\frac{1}{4}$, $7\frac{1}{2}$, $6\frac{3}{4}$,
4, $1\frac{3}{4}$ minutes to 3 o'clock in the afternoon;   then at 3 P.M., 1, $3\frac{1}{2}$, $5\frac{1}{2}$, $7\frac{1}{4}$ minutes
past 3, when I ceased my observations.

When one cell is completed the wasp goes in search of spiders, of which she generally collects from 15 to 22 specimens of three moderate-sized species. It is very seldom that any other species of spiders are collected. She takes them one by one and packs them half dead in the cell, being very particular as to the way in which they fit in. When the cell is full she deposits an egg, somewhat smaller than that of *Eumenes Latreillii*, and the egg is laid on one of the benumbed spiders.* She then closes the top of the cell with mud and commences a fresh cell at its side. She builds the cells in a row side by side, but the row is seldom straight, and she lacks that exactitude and neatness which characterizes the work of *Eumenes*. Sometimes, if disturbed, she will close a cell without putting in any spiders at all, and at other times she will only half fill the cell. The cell-wall attains a thickness of ⅜ inch. The wasp constructs from 10 to 20 of these cells in two rows one above the other, fills the interstices between the cells with mud, and smears the whole over with mud likewise, until it resembles a long lump of clay, and at this stage the nest is undistinguishable in outward appearance from that of the *Eumenes*. But if allowed to continue her work undisturbed, she goes a step further, and by means of diagonal streaks of mud gives the nest the look of a small piece of the bark of the common European Acacia. When laying on the mud, either at the very commencement or at the end, she works it by placing it on the required spot and then drawing it backwards towards herself, after which she runs to and fro over it, thus giving it the right shape.

When the spiders are all consumed the larvæ pours out of its mouth a dark yellow transparent material, which forms a shell around it, and looks much like goldbeaters'-skin : at the bottom of this shell is a hard black lump, and outside the shell are found the juiceless bodies of the spiders. There is no lining to the cell. Between this shell and the cell-wall a little fluff is formed, and this keeps the former in its position.

When the perfect insect is developed (it is not doubled up in its cell) it breaks through, and after cleaning itself flies away without any preliminary canter. I have not noticed whether on emerging the little drop of liquid is produced.

These wasps are terribly infested by Dipterous and other parasites, some of which appear to destroy the larvæ indirectly by consuming the prepared food (the spiders). With the flies the case is somewhat peculiar, as the mother insect appears to follow the wasp when she is carrying a spider, and deposits her egg on the food originally intended for the offspring of the wasp. I once found two and once five (Nov. 14, 1883) cocoons of these flies. In course of development the larvæ of these flies may be seen thriving on the spiders in the same way as the larvæ of the wasp ; but as they devour the juice of the spiders very quickly no food is left for the wasp's larvæ, which, being unprepared at that stage to develop unto pupæ, naturally die, and the mildewed remains of their bodies are found in the cell after their fully developed enemies have quitted it.

Another parasite appears to commence its attack on the insect itself in one of its more advanced stages. On one occasion I obtained three specimens of this parasite in its pupa-state. I found the pupæ inside the above-mentioned goldbeaters'-skin-like shell, so that the egg must have been deposited through the mud-

---

* Semon (p. 148, Engl. Edition, and p. 165, 2nd Germ. Ed.) says of a *Pelopœus* that she deposits her egg *in* the body of its victim. This cannot be, as the wasp has no ovipositor that would enable her to do so.

wall and shell on to the young wasp either whilst changing from the larval to the pupal state or when it had already been transformed into a pupa. The pupæ of these parasites are extremely lively.

SPHEX EPHIPPIUM, *Sm.*

These are underground builders. One which I observed on Nov. 4, 1883, emerged and brought up earth fifteen times in the course of eleven minutes. I once saw one pounce upon an insect which I took for a cricket. They cover up the opening of their nest every night when their labours are done. They are not particular as to site, sometimes mining under a shrub in loose garden soil, at others in the hardened ground of a well-trodden, but not gravelled footpath.

LARRIDÆ.

PISON VESTITUM, *Shuck.*, and PERPLEXUM, *Smith.*

The nests are exceedingly brittle, and are apparently formed of small particles of loose dry earth stuck together by some gummy fluid secreted by the wasps. They fill their nests exclusively with small spiders, and the larva makes itself a dull grey brittle shell in the cell. [The specimens to which this observation applies appear to represent two species; both probably have similar habits.—W.F.K.]

BEMBICIDÆ.

BEMBEX PALMATA, *Sm.*

These build underground nests.

DIPLOPTERA.

EUMENES LATREILLEI, *Sauss.*

Towards the end of last year (1883) I had an opportunity of observing how these wasps build their nest, at Mackay, Queensland.

As to the choice of position of the nest, I was unable to find out what the wasps preferred. The only nests I discovered were in out-houses on perpendicular walls sometimes high, sometimes low, and the presence of man (or bees or other insects) did not disturb them in the least while building. On one occasion I found a wasp building on a door of a shed which was in constant use.

When the wasp has chosen the spot on which she intends to build, she goes in search of water (either stagnant or running), but the particular one which I observed obtained water from the trickling overflow of a leaking pipe. She goes to the water and drinks, or rather takes in a supply, and then flies to a clod of not very hard clay-loam. With her mandibles and first pair of legs she scrapes up small particles of the clay, discharging water during the process. Before long she has made up a little mud-ball about the size of her thorax. This she carries to the chosen site, and commences work by making a little curved wall of mud as the basis of the cell. She then goes back to the water and commences afresh. The distance from the water to the clod was about 12 yards, and from the clod to the site about 4 yards, and it took her from 4 to 7 minutes to get her material, and she would then work from 1 to 2½ minutes. She appeared to have no difficulty in finding her way between the three spots, but occasionally she would try another clod; generally, however, she would come back to the original clod, which had a large and conspicuous moist mark.

Fig. 71, A and B, drawn to scale, gives very accurately the size of the cell as viewed from the side and above; also the various layers of mud as they were deposited, and which are distinctly visible to the last. When the cell was ready the wasp went in search of a common green caterpillar which infested all our vegetables, and put three of these (each about an inch long) into the cell. She carries these by the head, holding them with her mandibles and fore legs, and allows the rest of the body of the caterpillar to hang down in a line with her other long legs. She is very particular in packing the caterpillars nicely round the inside of the cell, and, if dissatisfied with her arrangements, she will occasionally take one out and adjust it afresh. When this is done to her entire satisfaction, she deposits one oblong light yellow semi-transparent egg, which is always hung by a light silken thread from the uppermost inside surface of a cell, whatever may be the cell's position. This done, she closes up the orifice with the usual mud, and commences a fresh cell by the side of the completed one. She continues thus daily building the cells, side by side, until she has completed about seven or eight, all in one straight row. She then constructs

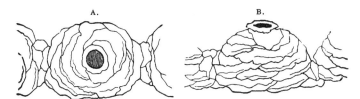

Fig. 71.—Nest of *Eumenes Latreillei.*—A, upper view; B, side view.

three or four, side by side, on the top of the first row; and, these being finished, she daubs the whole over with mud, ultimately giving it the appearance of an oblong lump of clay stuck on the wall, for by well smearing the mud she leaves nothing whatever to indicate the existence of the cells hidden underneath.

This wasp began to build on the 12th September, and finished on the 23rd of the same month, during which period she had completed a nest of ten cells. On the 3rd of November I slightly opened a cell which had been closed on the 20th of September, and found a wasp struggling inside. On the 8th of November I opened some other cells, and found several dead larvæ and pupæ which had been destroyed by parasites.

The cells are furnished with a silvery silk lining, with hardly any space between the lining and the cell-wall. This lining is fixed to the cell by fibres of a woolly appearance. In one corner of a cell, between the lining and the cell-wall, I found what appeared to be the cast-off skin of the larva, and excrements, as well as the skins of the caterpillars which had been devoured.

The wasps do not all emerge from the same side, some coming out at one end of the cell, and some at the opposite end.

On the 10th of November the wings of the wasp whose cell I had opened had grown to their full length, and on the 12th of November I let her out. She was doubled up, her abdomen being under her thorax, and she was working with her jaws, fore legs, antennæ, but there seemed to be no room for her to use her other legs. In the corner of the cell, inside the lining, was another cast-off skin. On the same day (November 12th) a wasp emerged from a cell closed on the 22nd of September, so that it would appear that it takes fifty-one days for the development of the wasp from the time the egg is laid until the wasp appears as a fully formed imago. Both the wasps on emerging emitted a few drops of a colourless fluid like water, and, strange to say, it appeared to me that this came from the thorax. Both wasps commenced to clean themselves as soon as they emerged, and then prepared to fly away, when I captured them.

ABISPA SPLENDIDA, *Guér.*

I found five specimens of these, which I took out of the nest. The larva and pupa develop without forming any shell. When the female has finished her nest she blocks up the entrance, but whether she destroys the approach or not I am unable to say. Each larva has a cell to itself.

[A short account of the nest of *Abispa ephippium*, Fabr., was published by Smith and Ker, Trans. Ent. Soc. Lond. (2) i. pp. 180, 181 (1850).—W.F.K.]

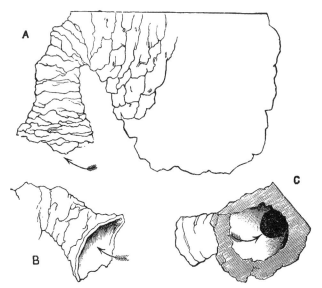

Fig. 72.—Nest of *Abispa splendida*. A. Side view, nat. size. B. Outer opening. C. Section showing the inner opening as indicated towards the point of the arrow.

RHYNCHIUM ROTHI, sp. n.

[Exp. al. 13-14 lin.

Female. Black; antennæ reddish, scape paler, bright yellow beneath. Head black; clypeus very finely punctured, wholly yellow, slightly angulated at the sides, rather longer than broad, and bifid at the extremity; base of the mandibles with a slight orange streak; hinder orbits and inner orbits from the clypeus to the depth of the emargination rather narrowly bordered with yellow, the intermediate orbits on the borders of the vertex very slightly marked with orange; vertex and thorax rather coarsely punctured; between the antennæ is a nearly equilateral yellow triangle, and two small oblique orange streaks lie between the two hinder ocelli and the front ocellus. Prothorax entirely yellow above; a small orange dot in front of the base of the wings; scapulæ black; meso- and metathorax black, the latter with three small spines at the lower angles. Abdomen black, the first segment narrowly, and all the others rather broadly, edged with orange above, and, except the first, narrowly below; the subterminal segment is more broadly bordered with orange beneath; and the terminal segment is entirely orange above, except at the base, and black, with a narrow yellowish rim, below; the orange border of the second segment projects forward on each side above, but the other borders are not perceptibly waved. Front legs reddish; femora black at the base, and with a yellow stripe at the tip beneath; four hind legs red, the greater part of the femora, the tips of the hind tibiæ, and the basal joints of all the tarsi black above. Wings yellowish hyaline, smoky towards the extremity; subcostal nervure blackish, especially at the base.

Male. The light markings of a much deeper colour, of an orange-yellow; clypeus (which is semicircularly emarginate at tip), labrum, and mandibles (except the tips, which are blackish) orange-yellow; upper part of the head almost entirely black; an orange-yellow mark, like a dumbbell, between the antennæ; orbits, from the clypeus to the depth of the emargination, narrowly reddish; cheeks behind the eyes entirely

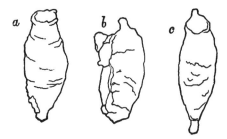

Fig. 73.—*a—c.* Outlines, nests of *Rhynchium rothi*, of natural size, and showing the irregularities in shape of nests made by the individual insect.

reddish on their lower portion, but this colour rapidly narrows, and ceases entirely at two thirds of the height of the hinder orbits. Prothorax and legs almost entirely reddish orange, the four hinder coxæ only being slightly marked with blackish; on the sides of the prothorax are two reddish spots and a streak, the uppermost and smallest of the spots being in front of the base of the fore wings. Metathorax very strongly keeled behind; sides orange, with a very strong obtuse projection. Basal segment of abdomen black at the base, red in the middle, and orange behind, the two latter colours not very sharply defined; a dusky line on the middle above, and a short dusky dash on each side above, near the extremity; the reddish-orange border of the second segment with a small black line in front in the middle, and a slight dusky mark on each side above; the borders of the remaining segments rather more extended than in the female, especially on the under surface. Subcostal nervure of wings not blackish, and tips of the wings less dusky than in the female.

Resembles *Rhynchium mirabile* and *R. superbum*, Sauss., but differs from both in the colour and shape of the clypeus. An unnamed specimen from Torres Straits, in the British Museum, appears to be a slight variety of the female, differing from Mr. Roth's specimen by its darker legs, and in some minute details of coloration on the head and abdomen.—W.F.K.]

The specimens herewith are, I believe, generally supposed to be distinct species, but as I have found them in the same nests, I am inclined to think that they are simply male and female. I believe these insects build nests like those of *Pelopæus lætus* (see Fig. 70). The cell is provided with a brown silky lining, in which the larva becomes developed. When the larva has shed its skin, the wings develop first, the eyes then gradually turn black, the abdominal bands turn dark as well as the thorax; finally, the legs aad antennæ become more defined, and the insect emerges fully developed.

ODYNERUS BICOLOR, *Sauss.*

These insects make use of forsaken nests of *Pelopæus lætus*, Sm.

VESPIDÆ.

POLISTES BERNARDII, *Le Guillon.*

These wasps build paper-like nests, suspended by a black stalk, and without any envelope. They feed their larvæ with a peculiar light yellow substance, which they collect in large lumps. A wasp, on arriving at the nest, shares this with the other wasps, who immediately set to work to feed their progeny. It is very droll to see the larvæ put forth their heads and greedily devour the food offered them.

HETEROGYNA.

FORMICIDÆ.

IRIDOMYREX RUFONIGER, *Lowne.*

These ants are very numerous and destructive at Mackay, Queensland, and attack anything and everything that comes in their way. They are not even afraid of the large species of *Camponotus*, some of which, when attacked, remain perfectly still, with a firm grip on the ground; but this passive resistance avails them nothing, for they are mercilessly dragged off all the same.

A tree in my garden (Chinese date-plum?) was infested to a great extent by green caterpillars, which appeared to feed at night-time, resting during the day under a web spun across a leaf. These ants discovered the tree, and cleared it of the caterpillars. Although they would sometimes enter the web to inspect it, they never attacked the caterpillar without first destroying the web, when they would bite the caterpillar till it wriggled out and fell among the ants below, who carried it off. These ants had numerous holes, communicating by pathways above ground, if not by subterranean galleries also, throughout the garden. They are one of the most abundant species of ant; and when alive are of a much blacker colour than when they have been preserved in spirit. They also milk the "waxy white louse" (pou à poche blanche) which infests the sugar-cane.

ŒCOPHYLLA VIRESCENS, *Fabr.*

They take possession of whole trees, gumming up the leaves for their nests with a white semi-transparent sort of paper. They rob beehives, not for the honey, but for the bees themselves. They go to the hive and attack the bees on their arrival. The latter have no chance against the numbers of the ants, and are stung to death and carried triumphantly off to the nests. These ants are very fearless and bold in attacking any one, and are armed with a very painful sting. I have seen them attack a *Curculio*, but the latter remained perfectly still till the ants left it, probably supposing that it was dead or unfit for food. If any one approaches a tree on which these ants are resting, they raise the front part of their body in a menacing manner. They are found on various trees, *Eucalyptus*, orange, &c., at Mackay, Queensland.

[Jerdon (Ann. & Mag. Nat. Hist. (2) xiii., pp. 104, 105—1854) gives a similar account of the nests of the allied Indian ant, *Œ. smaragdina*, Fabr., and says that although they feed chiefly on vegetable secretions, they are sometimes employed to destroy a nest of wasps that may have established themselves in a house. He does not speak of their attacking bees.—W.F.K.]

PONERIDÆ.

EUPONERA LUTEA, *Mayr.*

These marauding ants from Cairns, Queensland, appear to have no settled home, but roam about in masses, sometimes together and sometimes separating into small companies. They attack any insect they meet with, hunting their victims from under the bark of dead trees or out of crevices. Nothing comes amiss to them, and no insect appears to escape them.

CRYPTOCERIDÆ.

MERANOPLUS HIRSUTUS, *Mayr.*

These harvesting ants are found at Mackay, Queensland. They climb up grasses, and carry away the seed to their nests. The ground near the nest is generally strewn all over with the husks they have brought to the surface.

This is the end of the paper read before the Society, but with the corrections above referred to.

Fig. 74.—Pelopœus lætus.

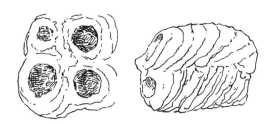

Fig. 75.—Nest of Pelopœus lætus.

To Mr. Rowland E. Turner I am indebted for the following notes :—

The commonest parasite on Pelopœus at Mackay was the beautiful blue-green *Stilbum splendidum*, Fabr., belonging to the family *Chrysididæ*; but I think they were occasionally attacked by *Leucospis*, sp., and perhaps by *Mutilla aurata*, Fabr., but I have no proof positive as to the two last. The caterpillars in the nest of *Abispa splendida* were sometimes parasited when brought in, and ichneumon parasite would develop, but, being unable to break through the nest, died.

" *Œcophylla virescens*, Fab., the green tree ant, is a great protector of the larvæ of *Lycaenid* butterflies. I have often seen several ants on a larva of *Lycaenesthes modestus* Waterhouse, they seemed to get some secretion they liked from it. The imago of *Lycaenesthes*, also of *Arhopala* and some other *Lycaenidæ* frequented trees in which the nests of *Œcophylla* were plentiful. The larvæ of the *Lycaenid*, *Utica onycha* Hewitson feeding on *Cycas* is similarly protected by *Iridomyrmex rufoniger* Lowne, and that of *Ogyris* by an ant of the genus *Camponotus*. The relation between ants and

Lycænid larvæ is well-known in other countries.   In examining the nests of ants in the Mackay district I was struck by the rarity of " Ant guests " that is of beetles and other insects living in the nests, usually on friendly terms with the ants.   Excepting species of scale insects and parasites of the genus *Eucharis* and allied groups I never could find any insect inhabiting the nests excepting *Lycænid* larvæ as above, though in other countries they are numerous.   I am inclined to think that my powers of observation were to a certain degree in fault, but I suspect that the tropical ants really have fewer domestic animals than those of temperate countries.   Nor could I detect any instance of keeping slaves.

" Honey pot ants are to be found at Mackay.   *Leptomyrmex varians* Emery stores up honey in the bodies of some of its workers which swell enormously though not quite as much as in the Mexican honey pot ant (*Myrmecocystus mexicanus*).   These honey pot individuals are not very numerous in the nest and, being only able to move very slowly, always remain at the bottom of the nest which in this species goes a foot or more below the surface.

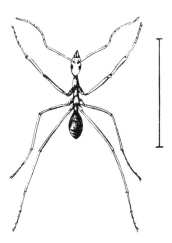

Fig. 76.—Leptomyrmex varians.

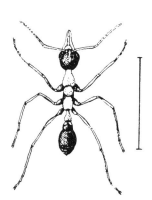

Fig. 77.—Myrmecia nigrocineta.

" The well-known ant *Myrmecia nigrocineta* Sm. has a habit of taking short leaps from one blade of long grass to another, thus saving itself the labour of descending. I cannot see that the legs are specialised for leaping.   This species when undisturbed makes mounds about a foot high in grassy country, but when the country is stocked with cattle the entrance to the nest is almost level with the ground without any mound over it.   If the cattle are taken off the land for two or three years the species again resumes its mound building habits.

" Fruit piercing moths, *Ophideres fullonica*, *O. maturna*, and *Mænas Salaminea* are very common.   They pierce the skin of oranges and other fruit with the tip of the proboscis which is specially adapted for the purpose and suck the juice.   I have seen as many as four of these large moths sucking one orange.   Other moths also visited the fruit for the juice but, as they have not the specially adapted proboscis and I was never able to see them piercing the fruit, I am inclined to think that they only make use of the holes made by *Ophideres*. Further north the splendid moth *Phyllodes imperator* Miskin has a very bad reputation as an orange sucker."

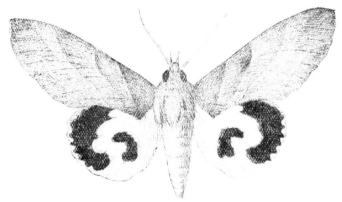

Fig. 78.—*Ophideris fullonicum*.

Lumholtz (*Among Cannibals*, London, 1889, p. 38) figures a hornet (*Mygnimia australasiae*) attacking the large hairy spider (*Phrictis crassipes*) which it had followed down into its hole.

Fig. 79.—Cane Carting at Glenalbyn (McBryde and Finlayson's). Hector M. Finlayson in the foreground in front of the cart.

14

Fig. 80.—Dr. Robert McBurney, affectionately known among his Mackay friends as " Plaster." Died at Samoa in 1899, on his way to England.

Fig. 81.—The " Leap " or Blackfellow's Leap, often miscalled Black Gin's Leap. It was an aboriginal man, *not* an aboriginal woman, who leaped over the precipitous side to escape from the troopers in 1867.

INDEX.

Fig. 82.—The " Amy Robsart " and the " Hannah Newton " at the site of the
Mackay Wharves, 1868.

PRINTED BY F. KING AND SONS, LTD., HALIFAX.